THE
UN GANG

THE
UN GANG

★   ★   ★

A Memoir of Incompetence, Corruption,
Espionage, Anti-Semitism, and
Islamic Extremism at the
UN Secretariat

PEDRO A. SANJUAN

DOUBLEDAY

New York   London   Toronto   Sydney   Auckland

PUBLISHED BY DOUBLEDAY
a division of Random House, Inc.

DOUBLEDAY and the portrayal of an anchor with a dolphin are
registered trademarks of Random House, Inc.

Book design by Michael Collica

Library of Congress Cataloging-in-Publication Data
Sanjuan, Pedro A.
The UN gang : a memoir of incompetence, corruption, espionage, anti-
semitism, and Islamic extremism at the UN Secretariat / by Pedro A. Sanjuan.
p.   cm.
Includes index.
1. United Nations. Secretariat.   2. Sanjuan, Pedro A.   I. Title: U.N. gang.
II. Title: United Nations gang.   III. Title.

JZ5008.S35   2005
352.11'3—dc22
2004065516

ISBN 0-385-51319-4

PRINTED IN THE UNITED STATES OF AMERICA

October 2005
First Edition

1   3   5   7   9   10   8   6   4   2

CONTENTS

The Bullies Blame
Their Victim

I n 1945, the victorious Allies created an organization, the United Nations, that was intended to protect civilization from another evil threat like that of the Nazis.

But the two superpowers that emerged from World War II soon did some rather stupid things.

First, they agreed to hold each other hostage by means of their increasing destructive capability, which could have obliterated all civilized life on earth. This awesome, mutually destructive power was to be monopolized by the U.S. and the USSR in tandem without letting the rest of the world have much to say about it. The survival or destruction of the entire human race was to be a bilateral affair that excluded the vast majority of the people who inhabited the earth.

Meanwhile, they had the gall to castigate any other nation that aspired to possess even a little weapon of mass destruction, an ambition that was hypocritically condemned as "proliferation."

Idealistic thinking had slid into blatant hypocrisy. Accordingly, neither the U.S. nor the USSR was to permit the United Nations to meddle in the vital issues of the Cold War, nor in anything that could affect the survival of the human race in case the U.S.-Soviet standoff fell apart.

The slow road to absurdity was therefore the only route left open for the UN. Over the years it grew into a convenient arena for the neutrals and the not-so-neutrals of the Third World to air their petty disputes and pretend to be involved in humanitarian causes.

After the demise of the courageous but meddlesome Dag Hammarskjöld, who died in a plane crash under somewhat sinister circumstances, the superpowers reached agreement on selecting candidates for UN secretary-general who not only came from weak countries, but were certified wimps as well. This allowed the bullying superpowers to declare that the UN could not get anything done because it was just a debating society.

But a debating society was precisely what the U.S. and the USSR wanted the UN to be.

There was thus no avenue of escape from incompetence at the United Nations. Incompetence was expected. Nobody with a serious plan for reform could get anywhere because the system was deliberately maintained in a dysfunctional state by the big powers.

Nevertheless, the UN remained a spiritual magnet for many who hoped that the grave social injustices of the world would someday be eliminated—problems like disease, poverty, hunger, mistreatment of women, racism, the plight of the handicapped, the exploitation of children. Much noise on these issues would be made by special UN agencies as well as at UN conferences and during sessions of the UN General Assembly.

Yet very little was accomplished by these well-meaning activities if we are to judge from the appalling progress today of AIDS and other vicious plagues, from the prevailing specter everywhere of famine and malnutrition, from the atrocious current plight of women and children throughout the world, from the widespread practice of slavery, from the continued increase in racism and religious intolerance, or from the rampant spread of genocide and terrorism.

As an effective political organ, the UN was controlled from only one place—the UN Security Council—where the superpowers held sway. There the U.S. and the USSR made deals, including choosing weak and ineffectual UN secretaries-general whom both superpowers could manipulate.

Meanwhile, the UN General Assembly, some of the UN's more politically active agencies such as UNESCO, and the UN Secretariat became ideological battlefields. The most important battles were for the loyalties of the Third World—those politically, socially, and economically developing parts of the world coveted as spheres of influence by the superpowers.

Intertwined in the East-West ideological contest was the war of the Islamic world against Israel, a conflict that was won hands down early on at the UN by Israel's enemies. The General Assembly passed a famous resolution equating Zionism with racism in 1975. At the UN, it appeared that the Nazis had expelled or exterminated Jewish racists and that the surviving racists had gone to Palestine.

The U.S. was Israel's greatest—and only—friend. But we had other fish to fry at the UN, and our diplomats were not about to take on the Islamic world over Israel on an either/or basis. It was enough that the U.S. supported Israel bilaterally with economic and military assistance.

The blatant and pervasive anti-Semitism at the UN was apparently regarded as a necessary evil of no great consequence by the U.S. government when the Cold War was at its height. After all, the UN was nothing more than a forum for venting grievances and for masking the dreadful international crime being perpetrated by the two superpowers, who continued for fifty long and anxiety-laden years to threaten to put an end to civilized life on earth at a time of their own choosing. Inexplicably enough, the U.S. government also turned a blind eye to the use of the UN Secretariat as a base for Soviet espionage activities.

But then the USSR collapsed after having drained its incompetent economy by pursuing an unsustainable arms race with the U.S. That has left the U.S. playing the role of the only superpower, or bully, as many UN staffers like to think of us.

The "natural" and long-condoned atmosphere of political anti-Semitism at the UN is now rapidly promoting the formation of an anti-

U.S., anti-Israeli coalition. This is happening regardless of the alliances and alignments the United States may be trying to maintain bilaterally or on a regional basis in different parts of the world.

The UN Secretariat has always been a political battleground. Should the UN Secretariat continue to operate as a covert arena for political maneuvering and disputes when it is supposed to be neutral, something it has never been? Is the present not a good time for the American people to insist on cleaning up the dirty politics at the UN, since the U.S. taxpayer is unwittingly funding anti-Semitism and a mindless form of anti-Americanism there?

The Secretariat has long functioned as a clearinghouse operation for Islamic extremist organizations devoted to the extermination of the state of Israel. Is there a way of coordinating antiterrorist law enforcement activities worldwide with an effective inspection of the goings-on in the UN Secretariat?

Are the causes of peace and world stability—ostensible UN goals—doomed to failure in a UN that harbors disruptive clandestine activities?

Does the UN have a value at present and for the future that transcends its inherited weaknesses? Most important, can anything be done to overcome the dysfunctional legacy of the organization?

My outlandish experiences as the "top American spy" for a decade in the UN Secretariat may provide some candid answers to these questions that go beyond the cosmetic reforms that are being introduced periodically.

CHAPTER ONE

So Your Father Was Jew!

So your father was Jew, yes?" United Nations Undersecretary-General Viacheslav Ustinov asked me abruptly.

He was a Russian who squinted constantly and spoke English with a forced, high-pitched voice and a persistent interrogative inflection. Instead of saying "er" between words, he said "myah." His eyes marbled off the wall next to him, cluttered with several pictures, poster-style, of the United Nations building and a large one of the Palace of Culture in Moscow. His shifting eye movements toward me and the wall seemed to be saying, "See? The United Nations may be in New York, but the Palace of Culture is in Moscow!"

Ustinov was the top Soviet official in the UN Secretariat, but not the top Soviet agent. His special assistant who watched over him held that honor, a fact that was well known around the corridors. Arkady Kashirin spoke and acted unmistakably as a member of the Soviet Committee on Government Security, or KGB. He would let you know with side glances and body language that he, Kashirin, was really in charge.

In a sense I outranked Ustinov, for I was understood to be the top American spy, a new commodity with my arrival at the UN. During the Cold War the Soviets had established a considerable covert beachhead at the UN Secretariat, and I had been unofficially appointed by Vice Pres-

ident Bush to monitor their activities. But I probably did not match
Kashirin, who held real power over Ustinov as a KGB control. I was one
against 274 of them at the time of my arrival, for, unfortunately, I was
the only American spy. I knew that all too well, as did Kashirin. Still, I
believe that he considered me to be some sort of worthy rival. We owed
each other professional courtesy as spies and scoundrels. During the Soviet era, no stigma was attached to being a scoundrel in support of the
right cause.

I had entered never-never land only a few days before, arriving from
Washington in mid-September 1983. It was not that I was unaccus-
tomed to circuslike environments, for I had already spent twenty-seven
years in the U.S. government, including time with several executive departments, two White House staffs, and an international development
bank—all organizations in which bizarre professional styles and equally
bizarre codes of conduct were standard. I had also spent a considerable
amount of time informally lobbying and appearing before the U.S.
Congress.

But the United Nations Secretariat seemed to me at first glance to
be a loosely supervised playground for alarmingly disturbed adults. Even
the Soviet staff members were allowed to engage in whimsical bureaucratic escapades provided they did not run away or defect. I was still too
narrow-minded and unprepared for so much lunacy.

Ustinov's question about my father's lineage was one that had never
been put to me while serving in the United States government. I asked
Ustinov to repeat the question.

"Your father, *your father*, he was Jew."

"My father was a Basque with a non-Basque last name. I don't believe he was a Jew."

"Yes, yes," Ustinov insisted. "Your father was Jew. I know. I have
very good sources in this building. You have a big file here at UN now.
Also, I have article—recent article—about you in newspaper *Washington Times*. It say your father was composer. I know!"

Several thoughts occurred to me during this seemingly demented
confrontation. Are all composers Jews? Was the KGB moonlighting for

the United Nations in Washington, stealing people's records for their UN personnel files? Why did my Soviet inquisitor give a damn who my father was? And more specifically, why was I—until a few days before an assistant secretary in good standing in the U.S. Department of the Interior—being subjected to this blatant anti-Semitic harassment? And why, indeed, was I being put in a position where I had to deny being Jewish in front of this idiot or anyone else?

But what I considered preposterous seemed to be a question of the utmost importance at the UN. Why was the United States sponsoring a Secretariat official who was also a Jew? Did it have any political significance? Was it a tangible and legitimate issue?

I quickly realized that haggling and lengthy arguments were the wrong strategy with the likes of Undersecretary-General Ustinov, who delivered an incoherent combination of smiles and intimidating expressions that did not appear to parallel his words.

"All right, my father was indeed a Jew, and proud of it, too!" I lied belligerently. Ustinov smiled very smugly, but gently, in what he thought was his moment of triumph.

But then he frowned.

"Yes, I thought," he said.

Soviet bureaucrats had to be right—always. I knew about that from numerous encounters with them in Geneva and other places during my Defense Department days. They would never agree with you. You had to make them think you agreed with them to get any point across.

Soon the mystery unraveled, however. The originator of another interrogation was not a Russian. He was a Peruvian.

Two days prior to my courtesy call on comrade Ustinov, I had visited the UN secretary-general, Javier Pérez de Cuellar, whose policy planning director I had been asked to become by means of an "urgent" telegram-contract from the secretary-general himself.

Don Javier, a Peruvian diplomat, was not much of a conversationalist. His occasional flair for subtle Cheshire cat humor later indicated to me that he was not stupid. Yet during social occasions he used to focus nervously on obvious trivia. At receptions he would say things like "The food is still warm at the buffet" or "So many people here are Polish," at a social gathering at the Polish mission.

"Your name is Sanjuan," Don Javier said at one point during that first meeting, with a slight interrogatory inflection. I had spent the previous first awkward minutes in a belligerent exchange with him, sitting on a couch across from his desk in his six-window office facing the East River from the thirty-eighth story of the UN—a great view except that much of the river traffic there usually consists of garbage scows. He did not look directly at me but in a glancing way, indicating that he saw me only peripherally.

"Yes, Sanjuan is indeed my name! I got it from my father, Don Javier. But then you have known that for a while now!"

"Yes," he replied, now gazing out the windows. "But how did you get the name of a saint? It is not very common."

"Well," I replied, "probably some ancestor of mine, way back at the end of the fifteenth century in Spain, converting from Judaism to Christianity, changed his name to San Juan as a sign of his sincere conversion, or so my father used to conjecture."

The secretary-general—apparently quite disturbed at the possibility that I was of Jewish descent—must have commented about the untoward discovery to a few of his aides. So at least the indiscreet Emilio de Olivares, Javier's assistant, suggested to me, apparently in an effort to ingratiate himself. Nevertheless, Olivares himself probably passed the alarming word around, "The Americans have sent us a Jew in disguise." And I was to be the top and only American spy with White House credentials. This was bad news. The news soon reached Ustinov, who confronted me with the "hidden facts" of my case when I paid him the courtesy call a few days later.

These Ionesco-like scenes did not take place in seventeenth-century Warsaw, nor in Minsk in the previous century, nor in the Kiev ghetto during the reign of Nicholas I of Russia. This was taking place in New York City in late September 1983, inside an international enclave apparently totally removed from the reality surrounding it.

For me it was the beginning of an anti-Semitic journey of ten years' duration that never ceased to amaze me, particularly after I realized that anti-Semitism was an established part of the UN way of life. It was not just a political attitude involving Israel. Anti-Semitism was a cultural mind-set, colloidally suspended or emulsified, that defined the UN "culture."

Yet this was not the only paradox that disfigured an otherwise benevolent and humanitarian UN image. Other quaint forms of racism as well as the indulgence of incompetence and sloth, along with a pervasive ecosystem of corruption, all competed for the UN malpractice trophy.

*   *   *

I had arrived at the main doors of that famous glass tower on Manhattan's First Avenue without a pass. It was a warm September day. My arrival was awaited in the office of the secretary-general with suspicion and alarm. The American spy was not welcome. The secretary-general himself was a former Peruvian ambassador to Moscow whom I had first met when I was a member of U.S. delegations dealing with the doomed Law of the Sea Treaty and the laws of war.

A uniformed guard had met me at the United Nations visitors' entrance. Tourists in shorts and sandals, some in pin curls with noisy children running around eating lollipops, were being allowed free access to the building. But not I, even on my first day of official duty. There was never much meaningful security at the UN, particularly in those preterrorist days. But the reception accorded to me was special. I seemed to be the present danger. Although I was actually already on the staff of the secretary-general, the guard escorted me in much the way they used with prisoners going to maximum security in Alcatraz. Still another guard halted me after I left the elevator at the thirty-eighth floor.

"Wait!" he commanded.

"Have you forgotten something?" I asked him quite audibly.

"What?"

"The word 'please,' my friend," I said, again just as audibly.

I told him I had no intention of proceeding anywhere since I did not know my way around and had recently been to the bathroom. He was not amused. Abruptly he pointed his finger to a place behind him by the windows that faced New York's East River.

I did not budge. Finally a secretary came up to me. She kept her eyes mostly closed, her eyelids strangely fluttering, I suppose to signify from the start her lack of patience with me. She did not ask me who I was. She knew who I was all too well. Apparently only I didn't know just exactly what I represented to the occupants of the thirty-eighth floor, the UN sanctum sanctorum. She must have sensed that I was an obvious, pulsating threat. Without a word, but by means of peremptory hand signals—emphasized by long, curving artificial fingernails—she led me to a narrow waiting room. I sat down on a leather armchair from which I could still see the huffy, claw-festooned secretary fidgeting at her desk.

My left eye caught hers. She came back to the door of the waiting room and shut it with unnecessary force.

"An auspicious beginning!" I thought. She soon reappeared and almost shouted with a British accent of palpable Argentine origin, "He will see ju!"

"When?" I asked.

"Immediately!" she blurted.

Before the nonsense about the origin of my name, Pérez de Cuellar appeared strangely taciturn, very shy, and, for some reason, somewhat embarrassed. He finally mentioned the weather. I instinctively looked out one of his six windows to verify the gibberish about the atmospheric conditions, and I realized that the helicopters making their approach to the heliport on Thirty-fourth Street were actually flying below the secretary-general's window, perhaps as a sign of homage.

"You were proposed by Vice President George Bush as director for political affairs. How do you feel about that?" the secretary-general asked me hesitatingly.

"Look, Don Javier," I replied, "with all due respect, I believe we both understand enough about politics not to treat this as some sort of job interview. I have a telegram from you that purports to be a full-fledged contract."

The secretary-general nodded nervously. Apparently he was not really a contentious man. He proceeded to show me his collection of Latin American art, most of which hung above the couch.

The title of secretary-general is confusing to many people. It means that he is supposed to be in charge of the UN Secretariat, which is in turn presumed to function as the UN nerve center. The UN General Assembly and the UN Security Council are roughly—very roughly—equivalent to the House and Senate. Thus the secretary-general is like a president—the person charged with implementing the laws or resolutions passed by the assembly and council and with taking executive initiatives as well. But this simple description would be misleading.

From its very inception in the mid-1940s, the UN was conceived as an organization where the victors of WWII would apportion real power among themselves while sharing certain seductive but ornamental functions with the rest of the world. Thus the UN Security Council was to deal with issues affecting security, as its name implied. On it, the uncomfortable partners in the grand alliance against Germany, Italy, and Japan had permanent seats and power to veto initiatives put to a vote. In fact, as the Cold War unfolded, there were only two meaningful participants in the Security Council—the United States, with its surrogates the United Kingdom and France, and the Soviet Union, with the People's Republic of China. Usually outvoted by the total membership of the Security Council, the Soviet bloc relied heavily on the veto for damage control.

The General Assembly, as its name implies, was very "general." There, all the UN member states had and still have one vote. Today the People's Republic of China, with a population of over 1.2 billion, has the same single vote in the UN General Assembly as does the Republic of Belau, created after a plebiscite I organized in the Pacific Trust Territory in 1983 when I was assistant secretary of interior. The population of Belau has exploded from 15,000 in 1984 to over 17,000 today. The concept of one vote per member state reflected the mind-set of the victors of WWII. Let the rest of the world have a forum from which to vent against or endorse the policies of the superpowers. UN General Assembly resolutions, of course, can have symbolic influence. In addition, the General Assembly carries out certain organizational functions that require perfunctory approval. But it is not and cannot be, under the existing representational apportionment, a meaningful world parliament.

The UN Secretariat is more than the administrative-executive branch of the UN. Implied in the concept that the Secretariat is to remain removed from the direct influence of the member states in its operations is an overall attitude of quarantine under which the most nefarious political stratagems are carried out along with the most outrageously corrupt practices, all under the cloak of diplomatic immunity and freedom from oversight.

During that first official meeting, Pérez de Cuellar, having gotten nowhere with his first approach, now tried a totally different tack. He explained that I was to direct policy planning for him and the Security Council with a staff ostensibly controlled by the Soviets. But, he added, in hushed tones, as if the walls of his office had ears (they probably did), that I would also be working as his liaison with the White House and U.S. Congress. He knew I had strong connections in Washington, and he expected me to use my good offices with Vice President Bush as well as with his "dear friend," U.S. Permanent Representative Ambassador Jeane J. Kirkpatrick.

In other words, he suggested that I, the "feared" American spy, should become a double agent. I remained silent.

I was soon to learn that the Soviets over the years had managed to maneuver, haggle, cajole, cheat, and bully themselves into many of the key positions in the UN Secretariat.

Although in the course of this narrative I will expose this network of Soviet control, I should point out at this juncture that the "Soviet" department of political and Security Council affairs, always to be headed by a Soviet undersecretary-general, was thoroughly controlled by the Kremlin through a system of Soviet assistants and KGB operatives placed in all supervisory positions. The large UN library was always headed by a Soviet librarian and the large majority of its staff consisted of Soviet officials. The secretary-general had a Soviet special assistant without a corresponding American aide. The Russian translation division, by far the largest group of translators and interpreters at the UN, was composed exclusively of Soviet-seconded personnel. In addition, pivotal positions in all other departments were reserved for Soviet-seconded officials, particularly in the administrative and personnel areas and in the vast Department of Public Affairs. All these positions remained under permanent Soviet control. Further on, we will see by what bureaucratic devices this control was brought about.

My State Department briefings had not included any details about the degree of Soviet hegemony in the UN Secretariat. Yet the Soviets essentially controlled the place with a regiment-sized staff and numerous surrogates from the rest of the Eastern bloc. Their official duties were often administrative, but their actual purpose was to protect a gigantic intelligence collection operation, which they ran under the cover of the UN. Their espionage efforts were directed almost entirely at the United States, called the "host country" in UN parlance—"host" in the same sense as a large organism is host to an infection. The U.S. Department of State had either ignored this Soviet undercover force or did not consider it to be of any importance.

George H. W. Bush knew something about this Soviet UN control system, not only because he himself had served as U.S. permanent representative at the UN, but also because he had followed Soviet intelligence-gathering activities closely when he served as director of the Central Intelligence Agency. When I collaborated with him at the American Enterprise Institute, he once or twice mentioned the UN as a center for Soviet espionage and was pleased when his colleague at AEI, Jeane J. Kirkpatrick, was selected by President Reagan as the US-UN permanent representative. Jeane felt all along that I should be inside the UN Secretariat because of my Soviet-area graduate studies background, my knowledge of Russian, and my more recent experience in different aspects of military intelligence. During my work as one of the coordinators of the Reagan-Bush transition team at the State Department, I had managed

Jeane's rehearsal and preparation for her Senate hearing as proposed U.S. ambassador to the UN.

Although I first accepted the position of assistant secretary of interior for territories and international affairs, Bush and Kirkpatrick waited until an important policy post in the UN Secretariat opened up before persuading the Reagan White House that I was the right person to become the first actual American spy at the UN.

Another Peruvian subsequently joined us during the first introductory meeting between Javier Pérez de Cuellar and myself—the secretary-general's top assistant Emilio de Olivares. For some reason he reminded me of Aramis in *The Three Musketeers,* sort of roly-poly but with eyes that betrayed a mean streak. Emilio and the secretary-general both made it a point to emphasize that they understood the need to check Soviet influence in the Secretariat. Underneath their "international" cloak, both of them claimed to support the United States and the West, something they harped on repeatedly to make sure I appreciated their friendship for the U.S. The secretary-general said, "We are all originally of European ancestry and tradition, after all—even you as a convert Jew."

"I am not a convert Jew, Don Javier. My father thought that he may have had a distant ancestor who was." The secretary-general gazed out of one of his six windows.

I believed less than 50 percent of the secretary-general's gratuitous protestations of love for America. I was overestimating.

★ ★ ★

"You are that fellow Sanjuan?"

I had now entered Brian Urquhart's office, the British under-secretary-general who had been described to me as an "institution," having been at the UN since its founding.

"Well, if you put it that way, I guess I am. I hope you are not disappointed . . . or whatever," I retorted—in a somewhat feisty manner, because the general reaction to me as a two-headed goat was beginning to disturb me.

"Well, your fame precedes you," Urquhart replied, all the while looking down at the floor in a token of well-bred British disdain.

"Tell me," he proceeded, "what was your role during the Spanish Civil War?"

My file, or what would be more properly referred to as my "dossier," was apparently being circulated throughout the upper levels of the UN bureaucracy. Those who had read the file and passed it along must all have been speed-readers, for the file, as I later learned, was about six inches thick and probably compiled over a period of several months in anticipation of my arrival. It was not compiled by the FBI, nor by the UN secret service—for there is no such thing—but in all probability by competent researchers working for the KGB within the Soviet staff in the Secretariat. They must have assembled a copious collection of (mostly trivial) documents and made the file available to the secretary-general as a courtesy, and he in turn saw to it that the bulging folder got passed around. It would have informed them that I had held a large number of government jobs.

I started in government as deputy chief of protocol in the State Department but working as Bobby Kennedy's "hatchetman," much to the discomfort of the staid Foreign Service bureaucracy. My mottled career as a troublemaker in the U.S. government subsequently involved a stint on the White House staff of Lyndon Johnson; then I became the nemesis of the president of the Inter-American Development Bank, a crook; this was followed by four years in the Office of the Secretary of Defense as deputy director for policy plans, deputy coordinator of the Law of the Sea task force at Defense, chief defense negotiator of the U.S. Chemical Warfare Treaty proposal, and chairman of the Defense Energy Task Force; then director for public affairs at the Arms Control and Disarmament Agency for two years; one year as the only Republican on the White House staff of President Carter; and three years as assistant secretary of interior.

In spite of Javier's pro-American protestations, I was nevertheless still the threatening intruder. Javier had probably shown the Soviets the reverse side of his coin of allegiance, how important he thought it was to keep American influence down at the UN. They were all Europeans also.

"My role during the Spanish Civil War? Well," I replied to Urquhart's inquiry, "let me see. I was the leader of one of the international brigades that fought against Franco. And, considering that I was six years old when that conflict started and eight when my family managed to leave Spain, I was, as you can see, quite precocious."

"Oh," said Urquhart with a frown. "Yes, I see. Well, your father was a musician, wasn't he? Did he know Gustavo Durán?"

Gustavo Durán had been a rather remarkable adventurer, a young composer by profession when the Spanish Civil War started in 1936 who joined the Spanish Republican military ranks, fought valiantly, and was gradually promoted in the field from enlisted man to general in command of a sector of the front in Cataluña. When the war ended, Durán fled to London, where he eventually married a wealthy Englishwoman. Subsequently he came to New York and joined the UN, apparently becoming a good friend of Brian Urquhart. My father, as a matter of fact, had known him in the 1940s when Durán moved about in New York musical circles.

"Yes, my father knew Durán, but in New York, not in Spain," I said.

"Ah, I see. But they were friends, I suppose," murmured Urquhart.

"Yes. I suppose they were," I said, "but are you trying to find out where my father stood politically during the Spanish Civil War? Was he a fascist or a communist? Is that it? Because if that is your intent, the answer is that my father, who is apparently getting to be well known here in the UN Secretariat, hated the fascists and the communists, and the socialists and the anarchists all equally and at the same time. He was a composer and a conductor, and all those insane warring factions in Spain were lousing up his career plans. My father was much more partial to Beethoven, Mozart, and Stravinsky than he was to Lenin, Hitler, or Mussolini. By the way, he knew Franco while serving in the Spanish army and was much later also a friend of Manuel Azaña, president of the Spanish Republic. Go figure, huh?"

I left Urquhart's office rather awkwardly. That was when I decided to take notes following all such further bizarre confrontations.

This was indeed a new experience for me after a twenty-seven-year career in the U.S. government. No matter how hostile the environment in Washington, this kind of third degree, this no-holds-barred grilling, was seldom if ever practiced.

My encounter with Brian Urquhart clearly illustrated the time warp at the UN. This British gentleman, this "institution" who had been recommended to me, was trying to decode my political DNA by referring back to "his" times, when postwar events finally led to the creation of the UN. The good times were during World War II, the antifascist struggle, and the liberal enthusiasm for a world order free from the black threat of fascism. Was I a fascist in disguise? That's what he wanted to know.

No, he had determined. I may have been a communist at an earlier time, as a child, perhaps, but not a fascist. Yet to him, who was nevertheless British, I was not a real American. Reagan should send as a spy to the UN a real American, surely not one who had played any role in the Spanish Civil War.

In a quaint sort of way, Urquhart was an interesting relic now deriving warm comfort from the protection afforded in an asylum for relics.

*   *   *

Mr. Videndra Dayal, *chef de cabinet* (chief of staff) of the United Nations Secretariat, put his hands together, fingers extended, and inclined his head forward—a common UN affectation—as he interrogated me during another ill-fated "courtesy call." Vindu, as his close friends called him to his face and most everyone else called him behind his back, was a small man with slightly bulging eyes and a distinctively British tailored look and accent who sported a strongly scented aftershave.

"Now that you are on the UN Secretariat staff, you may have to make a choice between your loyalty to the United States and perhaps to some other entity, and your loyalty to the secretary-general of the United Nations. Which way would you choose?"

First I was startled, then puzzled. The question was patently improper because it implied that in order to serve the United Nations adequately, an American had to be prepared to betray his own country. The secretary-general had already suggested that I do so by becoming a double agent. I was still suspected of being Jewish, and the "other entity" seemed to refer indirectly to Israel, since, as everyone knew, all Jews have a dual allegiance.

"Do you mean loyalty to the UN secretary-general or to the United Nations?" I asked.

"It is one and the same," Dayal replied, his head still tilted forward.

"Well, to me it isn't, Mr. Dayal," I said. "I wonder if you have put this type of question to any other recent appointees. Indeed, I wonder if you interrogate them at all. I fail to see how that choice would ever come up here at the UN Secretariat. The bottom line is this: If I ever faced such a dilemma, I would settle it easily by resigning."

Dayal was a morose critic of the United States who nevertheless considered himself a "neutral" observer. He proceeded to argue casuistically that everyone knew the Soviets had to operate by ignoring what they considered the temporary independence of any "international" organization. After all, in 1983 the Soviets and their surrogates were still anticipating the triumph of world communism and were therefore justified in not respecting the independence of any other world organization. Given their stated ambitions, it was simply to be expected that they would try to undermine the United Nations. On the other hand, Dayal made it clear that the case of the United States was totally different. We were a law-abiding (albeit "imperialist") nation whose citizens working in the Secretariat were expected to be perfectly behaved international civil servants and not spies or counterspies, which is how I was perceived.

Dayal obviously considered this definition of the different status of Soviets at the UN a rather clever way of laughing at the simplistic, noblesse oblige policy of the United States. The Soviets were not so stupid, he thought, but the Americans were.

CHAPTER TWO

Learning the Ropes

The reader may be wondering how the UN Secretariat, whose function is essentially to support the secretary-general, manages to employ over six thousand people at an annual cost that has long bypassed the $2 billion mark. We must therefore provide a brief survey of the Secretariat's highly redundant structure and staffing practices.

The putative nerve center of the United Nations is the UN Secretariat. Headquarters for the Secretariat is in mid-Manhattan by the East River. The operation is housed in a forty-story building, a well-known New York landmark, in two forty-story skyscrapers across First Avenue, known as DC-1 and DC-2, and in several large structures, such as the nearby former Chrysler Building, where thousands of additional square feet of space are rented.

In Geneva, Switzerland, a large complex that used to house the now defunct League of Nations as well as additional rented space now constitutes what is essentially a duplicate UN headquarters capable of servicing the requirements of conferences, the General Assembly, the Security Council, the Trusteeship Council, and the Economic and Social Council (ECOSOC), bodies that already have ample permanent facilities in New York. The Trusteeship Council meets only once a year for a few minutes in New York.

In Vienna, the UN has another near replica of its New York headquarters at the International Center, with an additional set of duplicate facilities existing next door, built by Kurt Waldheim, the crypto-Nazi UN secretary-general and later president of Austria. For a while he had dreams of moving the UN headquarters to Vienna.

In Nairobi, Kenya, the UN has yet another large facility, ostensibly to house its headquarters for East Africa, but also capable of doubling as a primary site for a UN headquarters.

In addition, the UN maintains conference centers in different areas of the world (the most well-known in Addis Ababa) as well as large operations in Paris, Rome, and Cyprus. At one point the UN also negotiated with Germany for the use of former Federal Republic of Germany facilities in Bonn.

In the principal capitals of the world and in the secondary capitals as well, the UN maintains additional ample facilities to house its United Nations information centres. The UNIC in Washington, D.C., is used as a headquarters for UN lobbying efforts before the U.S. Congress despite the fact that lobbying is a regulated activity in the U.S. capital, not permitted under the tax-exempt charter of any American not-for-profit organization.

In addition to these seemingly redundant facilities, the UN hosts a multitude of annual conferences in distant parts of the world (Durban, Beijing, Barcelona, etc.) that require facilities to be rented on a onetime basis for each conference. Travel expenses are a big item at the UN, with a budget in the neighborhood of $1 billion.

All these, and many other space requirements that fall into the miscellaneous category, constitute the permanent and movable physical plant of the UN.

What about the UN's approach to management?

Modern corporations and most departments or ministries in established governments throughout the world maintain charts that illustrate an organizational framework structured in depth. There is a top position, several assistant positions under that, then several subdivisions that function under the control of the top leadership and relate to each other as well. All such organizations are roughly structured in the form of pyramids.

Armies also are deployed in accordance with the principle of the pyramid, with in-depth defense and support capabilities. A linear arrangement without depth has been considered disastrous for any army since the days of Alexander the Great and even earlier.

Not so at the UN. There is a secretary-general, who has a so-called chief of staff, or *chef de cabinet,* in an office that houses several assistants without a direct line of responsibility or authority. Not too closely connected to the secretary-general and his staff, there is a wide front line of undersecretaries-general who perform many duplicative functions and yet do not relate to each other. The time-honored practice has been that, when there is some new function to perform at the UN, you create another undersecretary-general with or without another redundant department under him or occasionally her.

These undersecretaries-general are free to establish functions within their areas or departments that provide them with largely redundant services they do not normally expect to share with other undersecretaries-general. Thus each department has its own political affairs operation in spite of the fact that there is also a political affairs department at the UN.

There is no better guide to the bewildering proliferation of departments and agencies under the direct aegis of the Secretariat than the three-hundred-page UN telephone directory, or *repertoire téléphonique,* which is published in English and French, at the insistence of the French, their presumption being that French is still the international lingua franca. Here we are confronted with massive evidence of the kind of bureaucratic redundancy and overstaffing that would never be permitted in a public institution, let alone a private one, under minimal adult supervision.

Let us begin with the office of the secretary-general himself. The Executive Office of the Secretary-General shelters an assistant secretary-general for external relations. This is puzzling because the UN Secretariat consists of very little else besides external relations. The title in question is perhaps a disguise to cover the activities of a UN lobbyist before the U.S. Congress and various private, corporate, and public institutions. In other words, this is obviously a public affairs function.

In the office of the secretary-general there is also a director for African affairs. A director for communications carries out still another public affairs function, and another director has a "political affairs" function, whatever that might be.

There is an entire staff working for a spokesman in the executive office of the secretary-general, another public affairs function. There is also an "executive" office consisting of an executive officer and a squad of assistants. Yet the office of the secretary-general is officially designated as the "Executive Office of the Secretary-General." So one would presume, perhaps wrongly, that the whole executive office (of the secretary-general) would perform varied executive functions. What then does the "executive" office of the executive office of the secretary-general do? That is a puzzle.

Next among the sequence of entries we encounter the Office of Internal Oversight Services, with a well-staffed office of the undersecretary-general, but also housing another group of people who staff a separate executive office.

An internal audit division in Oversight Services consists of an internal section, a headquarters section, and several other sections, including a "field" section and, also, a separate African section, independent of the "field" section. The African auditing section has a headquarters in Nairobi, where some of the most glaring UN criminal conspiracies have been allowed to flourish.

During my ten years at the UN Secretariat, I was visited once by an internal "auditor." He began by asking me how many people I had in my political affairs domain and what their names were. I told him that the information he sought should have been well known to him before talking to me. I then suggested that he return to my office only when he was prepared to conduct a proper audit. I never saw him or any of his colleagues again.

All auditors investigate, but we find that Internal Oversight Services has a separate investigations division with its own subordinate offices spread throughout the world, one of which is in the Congo, with another in Nairobi. None of these activities seems to fall under another subcategory listed, that of field operations management. Puzzling . . . that these African field operations are not included under what is listed in addition as a field section or under still another separate African section also listed under Oversight Services.

Next we turn to the Office of Legal Affairs. Lawyers speak their own language, but most varieties of legalese are ultimately decipherable. However, in UN legal affairs, there is an office of institutions support under an already well-staffed general legal division and a publications operation with editors and copy preparers provided with an additional "legal" officer. This arrangement appears redundant and also bears a split-image-type resemblance to a public information function already performed in the Department of Public Information. A large complement of lawyers is housed under the roof of a division for ocean affairs and the Law of the Sea. Their activities relate to the Law of the Sea Treaty, which after decades remains unratified by enough significant UN member states to go into force and therefore is essentially dead in the water, pun intended.

Now comes the Department of Political Affairs. This is the basic political department in the UN. The UN is an organization whose functions are all generically political. So all the other departments of the UN Secretariat and other specialized agencies are also basically concerned with political affairs. Why a separate political department?

Here we find different regions of the world covered by a legion of UN staff members. Included are an Africa I division and an Africa II division and a separate representative office in Addis Ababa. An assistant secretary-general supervises the Americas, Europe, Asia, and the Pacific as well as an equally important Palestinian rights division. Also included separately is an undersecretary-general who acts as a special adviser for Africa independent of the Africa I and Africa II divisions.

Enter the Department for Disarmament Affairs. It has a regional center for peace and disarmament in—guess where?—Africa, of course! It also has centers (spelled "centres" at the UN) for Latin America and the Caribbean, but none for Europe. Europe perhaps is already either disarmed or altogether too well armed.

Now we come to the Department of Peacekeeping Operations, where there is also a well-staffed Africa division and other regional offices that duplicate the field offices of all the other Secretariat departments. Here there is also an office of the executive and still another, separate executive office, and an enigmatically denominated "Peacekeeping Best Practices Unit." There is not only an "office of mission support" but a "field administration and logistics division." There is a section of considerable size dealing with information management, which appears to be indirectly involved with public information. There is also a different administration and information management section and a staffing support section.

Another undersecretary-general heads the Office for the Coordination of Humanitarian Affairs, which has yet another Africa section as well as separate sections for all the other regions of the world, and still another section that deals not just with Africa, but also with Africa II, and, of course an advocacy, external relations, and information branch—that is, a separate public affairs operation. The humanitarian public affairs area is quite large. It includes an advocacy and external relations section, an information analysis section, an early warning and contingency planning unit, a field information unit, a relief web unit, an information technology section, an information technology support unit, and an information management/dissemination unit. Have we left anything out? Yes! An office of the representative of the secretary-general on *internally* displaced persons.

What about the Department of Economic and Social Affairs? That group boasts a budget and finance section, a personnel section, and a project finance section as well as a project personnel service—all matters that in a less sophisticated bureaucratic environment would be handled under a single department of administration—like the one the UN Secretariat already has.

Economic and social affairs also has its own information support unit separate from the enormously large Department of Public Affairs, coming soon in the UN directory. Economic and social affairs can also boast its own assistant secretary for policy coordination and interagency affairs—a very large operation with its very own development cooperation policy branch, among many other bland and fuzzy general captions and, of course, its own division for social policy and development, which encompasses an intergovernmental policy branch. Several telephone directory pages later this economic and social department winds up with a division for public economies and public administration, encompassing sections for public policy analysis, governance and public administration, public finance and private sector development, and, last but not least, an office of the special coordinator for Africa and the least developed countries.

The Department of General Assembly Affairs and Conference Services comes next with its very own central planning and coordination service, a large branch dealing with disarmament and a decolonization organs servicing branch, even if there is already a separate department of disarmament and no colonies in the world worth mentioning left to decolonize.

And then there is the largest department of all, with the unusually simple title of Department of Public Information. It has a staff of about one thousand engaged in communication and coordination, information technology, human resources management, budget, finance and general services, information dissemination, and its very own special public affairs division—within the public affairs department itself, that is. Somewhere in this spacious department there is a Palestine and decolonization section as well as a public liaison service, a special programs section, a users' services section, and an electronic resources development section. There must be a reason why the UN has to develop electronic resources.

The Department of Management has within its program (always spelled programme at the UN) a peacekeeping financing division and, naturally, an Africa section as well as Middle East, Europe, and Latin

America sections. Management also provides human resources management and supports the budget and planning of all other departments and offices and planning services as well as several clusters of specialized UN agencies that already have their own budget, planning, and human resources services, including an overseas service cluster (UNOG/UNCTAD/OHCHR/UNCC/ECE/ICTR/ICTY/ UNHCR/ICJ/UNOV/UNDCP/ECLACESCAP/ESCWA/UNON/ UNEP/UNCHS/UNCCD), all agencies that, naturally, have their own agency management facilities, coordinating facilities, and so on. The management department also flaunts an Office of Central Support Services with an information technology services division as well as an integrated management information service and a small security and safety service, perhaps in charge of removing debris after UN offices overseas have been blown up. Incidentally, the administration folks at the UN also have a United Nations postal administration that issues its own stamps, mistrustful as we all are of the unreliable U.S. Postal Service.

Other specialized agencies keep liaison offices in New York, Geneva, Addis Ababa, Nairobi, Vienna, and other locales, which coordinate with the UN's far-flung expediters and special coordinators. There are in addition independent regional economic and social commissions at the UN for Europe, Asia and the Pacific, Latin America and the Caribbean (a mild redundancy), and, of course, for AFRICA, and, in addition, a regional commission for Western Asia, which is separate from Asia as such.

Besides all the coordination that we have mentioned, there is a Secretariat of the UN System Chief Executives Board for Coordination and a UN Relief and Works Agency for Palestine Refugees in the Near East.

This is all separate from the United Nations Development Programme in New York, an agency with its own communications office, an enigmatically designated UN development group office, its own regional audit services with Africa headquarters in Zimbabwe, and its own program of assistance to the Palestinian people (PAPP). The UN Development Program (UNDP) has its own liaison office in Washington, D.C., due to the unreliable telephone communications system in the

United States, the fickle service of the New York–Washington air shuttle, and the infrequent train service out of Penn Station, otherwise an easy jaunt away from UN headquarters. UNDP has regional sections including one each for Africa, for the Arab states (the U.S. takes care of development for Israel bilaterally), for Asia and the Pacific, with a regional program division office separate from an overall regional program division. Subsumed under UNDP is the UN Development Fund for Women (UNIFEM) with its own geographic offices in Africa, Asia/Pacific, Europe, and Latin America/Caribbean.

The UN Population Fund in New York, almost contiguous with the offices of the UN Secretariat, has its own media services branch and, of course, its own geographic offices in Africa, etc., etc.

In the elegant nearby former Chrysler Building resides the UN Office for Project Services (UNOPS), a title that is not self-explanatory. UNOPS has its own divisions for Africa, Europe, Latin America, et al. In addition, project services has offices in Abidjan, Kuala Lumpur, Copenhagen, Geneva (good food there), Rome (even better food but more fattening), an additional Nairobi outpost, a Tokyo liaison office (if you like tempura), and a Washington, D.C., liaison office (mediocre food, but improving).

Although by no means a total picture of current Secretariat activities, the foregoing gives a comprehensive enough idea of how the so-called UN "system" maintains its integrity by not pandering to the limited notion of bureaucratic consolidation or adhering to a simplistic definition of functions that might have been designed so that a mere layperson could understand just what it is they do at the UN Secretariat. Yet it clearly illustrates the problems of redundancy, overstaffing, and paralysis by design.

*   *   *

Ensconced within the palaverous and extravagant chaos examined above, the division for political affairs I had inherited was supposed to serve as a policy planning arm of the secretary-general and provide a similar service to the UN Security Council. The Security Council, not being an executive organ, needed no such policy planning service, but the creation of an operation headed by an American had been a political compromise agreed upon long before my arrival to cushion the fact that a Soviet-controlled staff otherwise provided administrative support for the Security Council.

As director for political affairs, I had inherited an office of about twenty-five analysts and a clerical staff that was supposedly engaged in policy planning primarily for the secretary-general. All this was supposed to involve researching important issues looming on the international horizon that might be of concern to the UN Secretariat. The political affairs division was also supposed to help define overall policy for the secretary-general and identify troublesome international prospects.

Among the members of my staff were several Soviets, a few Americans, a Moroccan, a native of China who had murky citizenship credentials, a Filipino, a former Bolivian ambassador, a Polish chairman (on leave) of the Warsaw Communist Party, and a pompous Turk who described himself as the descendant of "generals."

After I announced that staff meetings would be held twice a week, protests immediately rang out. There had never been staff meetings before, all "my" people pointed out, and the Soviets complained that the meetings were an effort to "pick their brains," a practice akin to brainwashing, strictly forbidden in the Soviet Union.

"But you are not in the Soviet Union, you are at the United Nations," I observed.

"Yes, but we are entitled to behave according to our own proletarian tradition!"

"Very well, you follow your proletarian tradition," I said, "and I will follow my insidious American tradition. I will report you absent every time you miss a staff meeting. In the end you will win out by becoming true proletarians—that is, by being assigned duties with a broom sweeping the halls or with a mop in the restrooms."

A few days after this confrontation, I came out of my private office and tripped over a white-haired American squatting on the floor next to a bank of open file drawers, picking out stacks of items. He was a former ambassador who for years had worked in the office and had been described to me by Emilio de Olivares as "goody-two-shoes."

The Soviets had for a long time insisted that goody-two-shoes should have his appointment extended, for they got along with him terribly well. Indeed, they had excellent reasons to value goody's thoroughly submissive attitude.

"What are you doing on the floor?" I asked.

"I am taking some of my personal papers out of these file cabinets," he replied without raising his eyelids, burdened as they must have been by the weight of years of humble acquiescence.

"No, you're not! These are not your files anymore. They belong to this office. You had plenty of time to raid these files before you vacated the premises. Now, whatever you wish to have access to, please put it down on paper and, if I approve, my secretary will get it for you."

"May I see you in private for a moment?" goody-two-shoes requested.

Once behind closed doors, we did not have the showdown I anticipated.

He said, "It has been brought to my attention that you are thinking of instituting the American custom of staff meetings twice a week."

"I'm not thinking of instituting anything. The new practice has been announced, and we've already had the first meetings."

"Well, it is not the custom in the Secretariat to do that," goody kindly explained.

"You mean that even the secretary-general doesn't meet on a regular basis with his trusted lieutenants?" I asked, not willing to believe my ears.

"Not on a regular basis and not with all his trusted lieutenants. Here we value the judgment of professionals to determine their own schedules," goody said, looking quite satisfied with himself.

It did not take me long to ascertain that the status quo was precisely as goody described. UN Secretariat professionals marched to the beat of their own private drummer, or to the drum of their KGB handler. The titular chiefs designated to run the various departments and offices, and indeed the secretary-general himself, tried as much as possible not to interfere with each other or anyone under them.

Later when my UN office in 1988 produced a report about the impact on the NATO countries of national elections in France, a French assistant to the secretary-general intercepted it and sent it back to my office, labeling it unacceptable. I called her to tell her to mind her own business, and the French ambassador, Kemoularia, immediately sought an emergency meeting with Pérez de Cuellar. Kemoularia protested the abuse and threat to the psychological and physical well-being of a French national in the Secretariat.

Pérez de Cuellar, I was told by Olivares, cowered and promised to bring the matter up with me. Then he timidly asked me what I thought of the situation. I told him that papers from my office were for his consumption and to tell the French lady to mind her own business. I never heard the outcome, although I am sure that Don Javier reported to Kemoularia that the matter had been brought forcefully to my attention.

Such are the goings-on in the UN Secretariat, a collection of modern-day medieval fiefdoms over which secretaries-general have little hands-on control, and with which they have even less interest in tampering.

This enduring situation at the UN constitutes a badly controlled form of anarchy. It results in the most bizarre violations of the printed "rules of conduct" piously distributed every so often among the Secretariat staff to help perpetuate the fiction that the Secretariat is run like some normal organization headed by an executive who administers the rules.

In the past, the political affairs policy planning staff had been expected to prepare an occasional policy paper whenever their professional judgment indicated that they should. But their voluntary schedule had never required them to produce any systematic analyses. Inspiration was the primary source of motivation at the UN—a right won by all UN officials after many years of enforced inactivity.

I did not back down from my edict regarding staff meetings, nor

from assigning regular work responsibilities, including the writing of
policy papers about important issues that the secretary-general should
consider. The few papers sent by me to the Security Council were immediately returned with a note from the clerk of the council advising
that I was to be the repository and custodian of such papers, since the
rotary president of the Security Council, as this bureaucratic turtle
pointed out, was not an employee of the UN Secretariat, but a permanent representative of a member state.

Huh?

After a few months of this curious farce, I realized that forcing my
staff of anointed "professionals" to produce policy papers was a total
waste of time. None of the papers grudgingly produced under such un-
civilized duress was worth reading—first because the skimpy papers
contained no ideas related to what was going on in the world, and second because, having been mostly written by people for whom English
was a second language, they were frequently unintelligible. Eventually I
found a third reason to discontinue the torture—the secretary-general
himself didn't read our papers. Nor did he read the *New York Times* or
any other newspaper of record, foreign or domestic, except an occasional copy of *El Tiempo* from Bogotá, admittedly the best paper in the
Andean republics. His trusted assistants—three fellow Peruvians—took
care to keep Pérez de Cuellar up to date on current events by word of
mouth, in a process otherwise indistinguishable from idle gossip.

A few months after my arrival at this palace of sloth, I noticed my
Moroccan colleague tiptoeing out of an elevator at the Secretariat entrance and skulking mysteriously in covert pursuit of somebody ahead
of him.

I hailed him.

"There she goes again!" he exclaimed. "Filipina, my secretary, not
out to lunch, but out to Bloomingdale's. Three hours for lunch! And she
won't type or even answer the telephone because she is usually polishing
her nails. Can you imagine that?"

"I can imagine that, my friend. But if she is really that bad, then let's
fire her."

"You must be joking!" he choked. "You don't fire secretaries in the UN. They come in with a one-year temporary contract. At the end of one year of marginally acceptable behavior, they get a permanent contract—and after that they are on board for life."

I was curious about this arrangement since I myself had no fewer than ten secretaries under my aegis. So I called the director of personnel, Monsieur Nègre, who confirmed what my colleague had said. When I asked him about it, the director explained his inability to fire a permanently employed secretary as a perfectly normal organizational policy that, surely, everyone could understand.

Later on, Kofi Annan, who became the next director of personnel—now the secretary-general, the only type of secretary who can be fired at the UN after his five-year term expires—confirmed the subtle nature of the UN cradle-to-grave tenure policy covering clerical staff members. Not only could they not be fired for anything short of overt criminal behavior, but he advised that, if I wanted to move any duly consecrated secretary out of our office, the trick was to give her consecutive performance ratings at the highest level so that some sucker heading another department would be snookered into taking her. If you were to give her an inferior evaluation, Kofi warned, you would be stuck with her for the duration of life on earth or until her retirement—whichever came first.

As the months passed, I began to reconcile my marginal U.S. government scruples to this new-to-me international civil service arrangement. My arrival at work at 9:00 A.M. was unnecessary since the troops showed up at 10:00 or 10:30. So did the secretary-general. I got to the office before 9:00 only because I drove my wife to her office, and she worked in the local New York economy. One-hour lunches were merely hypothetical since two and a half or even three hours was the accepted and honored UN practice. Departure from the premises after 5:00 P.M. was considered punitive. Most people were gone by 4:00.

And why not, after all? The work performed by the gallant inmates of the Secretariat was the product of a blurred commitment, an ill-defined obligation of a very personal nature. It could not be limited by artificial, inflexible restraints.

"This is freedom, what we practice at the UN," my Moroccan assistant said, clowning around. "You Americans are always talking about free this and free that. Well, you should understand how we treasure our freedom at the UN. This is not a dictatorship."

It was in this grotesque bureaucratic environment that the daily business of the Secretariat was conducted when I arrived at the UN, and, absent any subsequent serious and thorough reform of the system, it is very much the way the place is still being run. Yet within this outlandish make-like-you-work setup, the real business of the Secretariat, the political machinations of the Soviet Union and Soviet bloc countries as well as the lesser intrigues of other member states, was conducted under the impenetrable camouflage of a web of ingenious bureaucratic fabrications.

Let us examine how the Soviet mafia operated in this paradise for spies.

CHAPTER THREE

The UN Soviet Mafia

Much earlier, when I worked in the U.S. Department of Defense, I was subjected to security training sessions, and some simple procedures have always stuck in my mind. Every time I occupied a new office, I would check the telephone for listening devices or bugs. In those still-primitive days of the twentieth century, this could be done by simply unscrewing the mouthpiece and earpiece and looking inside for any device that did not seem to belong there.

After being introduced to my United Nations four-window office with its view of the East River and the large Pepsi-Cola sign that festooned Long Island City, I proceeded to check my telephone. I felt that in this international environment there might be some reason to be suspicious, although I also chuckled at my sinister apprehension. There I was playing spy!

I did find something strange inside the telephone receiver, but it was not a listening device. It was a small plastic bag of white powder.

I contemplated what I should do, and then I thought about what I could do.

The UN environment was decidedly hostile. That was no delusion. I was regarded by the Soviets as a particularly unsettling enemy. Had I any witnesses to the fact that I had found the glassine envelope inside the phone? No. Could the little packet have been left there by my predecessor? Unlikely, for he had vacated the office weeks before I arrived. Could some secretary or member of my staff (I still hardly knew all their names) have placed the envelope in my receiver for subsequent personal use? Also very unlikely, for that would have made gaining access to it much more difficult. Was it an intentional practical joke? Also unlikely, for people do not normally take telephones apart, as I did. Was it meant to be found during a UN security search a while later, after I had been in office a few weeks? That seemed more likely.

I decided to slit the bag, take a very small sample, and wrap it in a piece of toilet paper. Later I threw the bag and the rest of its contents into a toilet in the men's room. I had the small sample tested through reliable channels.

It was powdered cocaine of a superior grade.

My first impulsive reaction was to protest what was an obvious dirty trick and lodge my protest with the secretary-general himself. Calmer judgment prevailed, however, and I brought the matter up with the security people at the U.S. mission instead. They smiled and informed me that things like that happened all the time in the UN's diplomatic ecosystem. I was advised to just keep my eyes open.

Advice of that nature I did not need, so I returned to my original plan and mentioned the infuriating incident to Don Javier two days later in his office. The secretary-general called in his right-hand man, Olivares, and they both informed me—in strict confidence—that such a trap was one that only the Soviets would set. Olivares helpfully explained that there were some Russians around who probably belonged to the Soviet "secret police" or KGB!

I found this scene—which was acted out with straight faces—to be worthy of a Restoration comedy, so I decided to participate in the farce. After a meeting with the Soviet undersecretary-general—the already introduced Ustinov—I asked him to get his nominal subordinate Kashirin into his office. Naturally I did not refer to Kashirin as Ustinov's KGB control, for stating the obvious can sometimes create unnecessary resentment.

I told them the entire story, emphasizing the interpretation given to me by the secretary-general and his sidekick Olivares. Ustinov's eyes opened wide and then he frowned. Kashirin on the other hand broke out in laughter, and I laughed with him. Ustinov seemed disoriented.

Finally I said to Kashirin, "Don't tell me you think it was actually planted by the FBI trying to test my ability to react under stress."

"Yes," said Kashirin, "konyechno," or "of course."

This farce accomplished at least a double purpose—to get the Soviets mad at the secretary-general, who was playing both sides against the middle—and perhaps to notify the secretary-general that such silly tricks would not work, in case he had been complicit in the stratagem.

Last, it made me lighten up a bit more.

One day I stayed home to nurse a nasty flu. My phone rang, and a bizarre conversation took place between me and what was then the New York Telephone Company.

"Hello, this is the New York Telephone Company. Is this a private phone or a business phone?" I was asked by a male voice.

"You ought to know. You are the ones who bill me!"

"Well, at the request of a client, we are checking on long-distance telephone numbers called from a number at the United Nations."

"And who is that client?"

"It is the United Nations."

"Who in the United Nations?"

"I am not permitted to give out such information."

"And I am a lawyer," I equivocated, "and the freedom of information and privacy laws applied by the Federal Communications Commission require that you give me that information on request. You want to go to court?"

"It was a certain Boyer, who has asked us to check the long-distance numbers called from 212–963–5486," the voice replied. That number was mine at the UN.

From the courageous Moroccan on my staff, who hated the Soviet UN superstructure, I learned that the administrative manager of the Department of Political and Security Council Affairs was a Mrs. Solange Boyer. She had an active French communist background and was a favorite protégée of the Soviet undersecretary-general.

Ustinov apparently wanted to know whom I was calling in Washington. I lived in Westchester County, technically a long-distance call from Manhattan. Obviously Ustinov did not realize that my home number was listed as a long-distance number on my UN telephone bill and that I would answer it. I believe Ustinov was particularly interested in my contacts with U.S. senators and congressmen. I might also be calling a number of other interesting Washington offices. The New York Telephone Company was unwittingly performing an espionage function for the KGB.

The next day I called Mrs. Boyer into my office and confronted her with the particulars of her clumsy investigation.

She replied, "In the first place, Mr. Sanjuan, I have nothing to do with the New York Telephone Company. In the second place, tracing your long-distance calls is perfectly in line with the UN's responsibility to see that you do not use your phone for calls that are not official."

Her answer had the Alice-in-Wonderland ring to it that I was beginning to associate with most official UN business.

"All right, madame, now you listen to me very carefully," I replied. "Take down these two numbers: 202-224-3121 and 202-395-2000. The first is the operator in the United States Capitol, through whom I will henceforth reach any senator, congressman, congressional committee, or congressional staff member I wish to talk to. The other connects with the White House 'signal' operators. The operators there remember me as a former member of the White House staff. Those operators will connect me with anyone in the executive branch of the U.S. government whom I need to call, or with any synagogue, temple, or mosque I desire to reach, even with any movie theater or supermarket. Anytime your Soviet control officers want to know whom I have called in Washington, tell them to see me, for those two numbers won't be of much use to you no matter what connections you may have with the New York Telephone Company. Now—in the second place—if you pursue any further inquiries into my official or private affairs, I will issue a well-documented complaint to the U.S. mission to the United Nations about your espionage activities, with a copy to the FBI, another to Mr. Richard Bernstein, who covers the

United Nations for the *New York Times,* and two further copies to the chairman and to the ranking minority member of the Senate Intelligence Committee. I feel confident that the UN secretary-general will reluctantly understand the need to send you back to France, where you can again take up your activities with the French Communist Party."

I felt sure that all hell was going to break loose shortly after this exchange and that Undersecretary-General Ustinov would at least claim that he could not tolerate interference in his department by a confrontational American like me. But weeks passed and nothing happened.

How did Madame Boyer operate? Well, she was in charge of the Office of Administration inside the UN Political and Security Council Affairs Department, headed by the aforementioned Ustinov, and completely controlled by the Soviets. What administrative functions did she actually perform? Essentially none, except to maintain some superficial liaison with the UN Department of Administration, which handled all personnel records, travel budgets, performance evaluations, and other perfunctory services required in any large organization.

Madame Boyer, of course, had significant close contacts with seconded Soviet UN officials in the Administration Department. They would provide her with records on any member of the Political and Security Council Affairs Department and on any other official in the UN Secretariat, including the secretary-general himself. She got anything that Ustinov and the top KGB types (Kashirin and his boys and girls) wanted to see.

Madame Boyer also handled KGB relations with the outside world, mostly with New York City officials and large public utility services like the telephone company, or the airlines, or the UN travel agency—all for the purpose of keeping tabs on anybody in the Secretariat her Soviet boss wanted to know about. In other words, Madame Boyer, with her heavy French accent, masqueraded as a legitimate UN administration official while actually functioning as a Soviet spy.

The first positive reaction to my "porcupine" behavior was an invitation to lunch from Arkady Kashirin, the special assistant to Undersecretary-General Ustinov and the KGB guard dog who kept an eye on his purported boss.

Ustinov's precursor, Arkady Shevchenko, had defected from his post in 1978 and obtained political asylum in the United States. A mousy little man with a gift for telling Americans that they knew nothing about Russia and were running their own government all wrong, Shevchenko had settled in Washington and quickly written, with the expert assistance of his new American wife, a memoir entitled *Breaking with Moscow,* the riveting message of which was that the Soviet Union was dangerous. His Russian wife and children he had conveniently ditched in Mother Russia. The Soviet government had thereafter placed KGB mastiffs around Shevchenko's UN successor to see that neither Ustinov nor his staff got any bright ideas about emulating Shevchenko's example.

My inquiries about Kashirin's real credentials had been relayed to the CIA and FBI. After twenty-seven years in the U.S. government, I had many reliable contacts outside of the State Department. Kashirin was identified for me as officially with the Foreign Ministry in Moscow, seconded to the United Nations Secretariat, but the information was accompanied by the caveat that he was probably at least a colonel in the KGB.

"Pyedra . . . may I call you Pyedra?" Kashirin, who had behaved somewhat stiffly for weeks, now unctuously asked as we faced one another in a second-rate Chinese restaurant on Second Avenue. Chinese restaurants were the favorite of many Russians at the UN, because, as they frequently said, "Chinese food is always good."

Kashirin, who had a natural wise-ass look about him, faced me with a half smile that showed he doubted everything I said. He was, at the same time, constantly curious about my own "hidden" sinister purpose, which, of course, was to find out what shenanigans he was up to.

Our conversation was diplomatic, which is to say topically inane, for we both avoided saying anything compromising. I mused as to what passersby on the street (we sat near a window) might think we were doing since we were not saying very much but smiling a lot in a very meaningful way. A dialogue of many smiles without too many words, with long pauses filled with "hmm's" and "I see's."

After sparring in this manner throughout our two-course meal of mediocre shredded beef and crispy fish, including dessert with fortune cookie, the time came to pay. My order plus soup, appetizer, Heineken beer, and a fancy banana flambé with ice cream apparently amounted to much more than the cash Kashirin had been awarded at the Soviet mission, even for a KGB-sponsored lunch.

"What's the matter, comrade?" I asked as he looked at his wallet with a troubled expression. "Didn't you get enough money from the Soviet mission?"

"No, it is my money! Like you, I too make money at the UN!"

"Yes, of course! I don't doubt that. But, you know, they'll actually take your credit card here. You have American Express, don't you?"

"No, in the Soviet Union we don't have American or Russian Express. We do not believe in credit cards. It is a bad capitalist habit that benefits your Jewish moneylenders. Do you know that the head of American Express is actually Jewish? Borrowing gets you quickly into heavy debt," Kashirin protested with a vengeful leer, knowing damn well that I knew the real reason why he did not have a credit card to his name. The Soviet government didn't allow him or any other Soviet UN official to have a credit card in order to make defecting more difficult. I wondered who was looking over Kashirin's shoulder.

Besides such handicaps, all Soviet functionaries were bound by even greater shackles that reduced their living style to the level of extreme frugality and even penury. All Soviet staff members, who were paid the UN's fairly generous salaries (at least 25 percent of which was contributed by American taxpayers, of course), had to kick back about 75 percent to the Soviet government. In exchange they got "free" but lousy Soviet mission infirmary medical service, heavily subsidized housing in a jail-like compound in Riverdale, and free Russian school facilities for their kids. All the benefits they put in for and got at the UN—tuition subsidies and reimbursement for rare New York doctor's visits, UN housing subsidies, and paid home leave—they also turned over to the Soviet government. Thus, the poor souls lived like paupers, and even the numerous KGB agents in their midst had to get cash from the Soviet UN mission for approved lunches.

For fear that those susceptible to the venal lures of the American way of life would be tempted to take the short yellow road to capitalistic freedom, the Soviet government did not allow its UN staff members to apply for American credit cards. Any of them could have easily gotten one given their generous, albeit hypothetical, UN salaries. The penalty for breaking these rules was immediate return to the Soviet Union regardless of the amount of time remaining on the normal Soviet-seconded UN contract, which on the average lasted two years.

The Soviet government was therefore making a nice capitalistic profit out of its UN agents while discouraging Soviet UN staff from living with too much dignity in the decadent land of plenty.

The UN Secretariat collaborated with Soviet authorities by immediately firing any Soviet-seconded employee whose appointment was withdrawn. Poor, without credentials, without a job, any Soviet maverick would have a difficult time avoiding the authorities from the Soviet mission in New York in order to seek asylum in the United States.

Kashirin again looked at the bill with patent anxiety and then looked at his thin wallet. I took out my wallet, pulled the bill out of his hand, and said, "Let me have the pleasure." He heaved a sigh of relief in his human, non-KGB capacity. As I flipped my wallet open to retrieve my American Express card, Kashirin noticed a big gold badge pinned to the inside that had engraved on it, amid starlike rays, Micronesian Bureau of Investigation.

"What is the badge?" Kashirin asked, noticeably startled, looking into my eyes intently with an expression of alarm.

"Oh, that is because, when I was assistant secretary of interior, I helped create the Micronesian Bureau of Investigation in the U.S. Pacific Territories to hunt down drug dealers. I was made honorary chief of the bureau, and I still am. It's good for life actually. I am very proud of it. I am also, by the way, a major in the Guam police and a captain in the Virgin Islands police. This badge gets me all sorts of professional courtesies from the NYPD and from any police department in the entire United States. It worked wonders for me in Washington. It is not entirely honorary, though. I also carry a copy of the commission in another wallet compartment, and I have the right to give 'hot pursuit' to any Micronesian criminal loose in New York. But, believe me, Arkady, I wouldn't dream of chasing any Micronesian anywhere because they are a very physical people and rather dangerous when cornered."

Almost immediately after that lunch, I had a call from my other Soviet pal, Undersecretary-General Ustinov.

"Would you have with me lunch?" he asked.

The very next day we went to an Indian restaurant half a block from the UN.

Ustinov beat around the bush with almost rhythmical syncopation during our lunch. Did I like Indian food better than Spanish food? Why did the United States oppose the Law of the Sea Treaty? Wasn't New York, which was so humid, really colder than Moscow? Finally, he asked, "Oh, do you have police badge?"

"Oh, yes," I answered. "I have several. Do you want to see the one in my wallet? It is very pretty."

I let him admire the badge, but I did not release the wallet. Ustinov finally paid for the puri and masala. He even left a tip!

There were to be more lunches with badge-fascinated Russians. One, a certain Perevertsev—whose proposition ranked fifth in the order of invitations I accepted—unceremoniously let me pay the bill at the Soviet-accredited Chinese restaurant on Second Avenue. Perevertsev was an engaging KGB scoundrel who spoke fluent English and enjoyed playing riskier games than his other colleagues in the Soviet intelligence profession. Other KGB and GRU (military intelligence) types liked to play cat-and-mouse, but Perevertsev had a taste for cat-and-cat.

"So, all my compatriots tell me you have a very pretty badge that gets you out of parking tickets in New York. Is it as harmless as you pretend?"

"How could any badge, particularly a legitimate honorary badge like the one your buddies have seen in my wallet, be harmful, tovarisch?" I retorted.

"Do you mean by *tovarisch,* or what you call comrade, to intimate we are in the same profession, you and I?" Perevertsev asked with an openmouthed smile, one eye shut, and an audible snort, to emphasize, I suppose, the metaphorical nature of his question.

"Why, old boy, we are both international civil servants, of course! What else could you have in mind?"

"But you were a deputy minister in your American ministry of internal affairs, am I not right?" Perevertsev parried in the second or third fencing position—I'm not sure which.

"The Department of the Interior is not our ministry of internal affairs as is your Ministerstvo Vnutrenych Del'. Ours deals with natural resources, rivers, forests, mines, national parks, territories. Internal in that sense. We don't take people to Lubyanka prison," I said putting on a mock-serious face.

Perevertsev grinned widely to signify he thought he now had me trapped. "But you have the Park Police, don't you? And they deal with your FBI, and you are the honorary chief of the MBI, which, if I am not mistaken, is Micronesian Bureau of Investigation. No?"

"So, as far as you are concerned, this is the KGB having lunch with the MBI, right?" I laughed.

"How do you know I am KGB? Maybe I am GRU, you know, military intelligence, or maybe I am just innocent fellow coming from a poor country that is always terrified of being invaded by Tartars, Poles, Turks, Jews, Swedes, French, Germans, and Germans all over again. You Americans don't get invaded. You invade, but only for the good of the natives."

There was poignancy in what he said. Such was often the typical last resort of many Russians I have known who are driven to use the "poor little me" defense to justify themselves.

I thought that the exchange had been worth the price of the mediocre Chinese lunch, so, as I said, I took the bill.

Later, while sitting in my four-windowed office overlooking the East River, beyond which spread a very American panorama—Long Island City, Queens, Brooklyn, and, further, the New York airports and segments of Westchester County, all visible, if I strained, from the thirty-second floor of the UN Secretariat building—I wondered about my present convoluted and incongruous situation. I was being repeatedly scrutinized and interrogated in the course of multiple mediocre lunches. I was being exposed to the most blatant variety of overt anti-Semitism.

All of this was happening because I had been identified as a loyal American right here, in New York, and I was also suspected of being a Jew.

Undersecretary-General Ustinov next approached me after a meeting with the secretary-general and asked, "You have not yet sign contract at UN?"

"I believe the secretary-general's telegram is a contract," I replied.

"You have not sign telegram?" he asked again, with a very appropriate, friendly smile.

"No, I signed for the telegram, but, as I believe you know, one cannot sign a telegram. I have no reason to doubt that there will be an official contract, do you?" I asked.

"How you say, 'There is many lip between slips'? Is that right?"

As each day passed, I continued to marvel at the discourtesy and defiance I was meeting. Some of it, I was sure, resulted from the customary disrespect with which United Nations officials treated each other, contrary to the popular image of the United Nations as a place of high protocol and elegant diplomatic manners. But a good deal of the face-slapping was expressly directed at me, the assertive American intruder, the interloper—the spy. And, oh yes, the undercover Jew! This was the UN way of grudgingly putting the United States in its place.

To cope with this recurring antagonistic reception, I decided to give back twice as good as I got, reasoning that such an attitude would project an image of someone who felt secure about his outside support.

So, to Undersecretary-General Ustinov's unsubtle hints that I perhaps would have no contract, I replied:

"The cup had better connect with the lip, Slava. Otherwise, if I were you, I would rush to the United Nations Credit Union and get a short-term loan to tide me over."

"Credit? What is meaning of credit for this?" Slava's steadily improving English suddenly had the sputtering fluency of a faucet right after the plumber has turned the water back on.

"Well, it's like this," I answered. "If I had no contract, my friends back in Washington, not only in the White House, but in the Congress, would get very upset. This year's United States contribution to the

United Nations budget would be at least considerably delayed, if not withheld. Then the United Nations secretary-general would not make payroll. And you would need a loan to tide you over for a few months!"

Soon after that friendly exchange, I said to myself, "What the hell, where is my official contract?" And, with this question on my mind, I went to see the director of personnel, the aforementioned Nègre. I entered the personnel director's office at the suggestion of his secretary, but the director was pretending to read some document, the pages of which he was not turning.

"Yes?" he mumbled after a short while, without taking his eyes off the prop he was holding in front of his face.

I said nothing.

He mumbled "Yes?" again.

"Customary courtesy requires that you put down that document, that is, if you and I are going to talk to each other here. If not, we can meet in the office of the secretary-general, where I presume you will not be pretending to read a document."

The director of personnel informed me that contracts took a long time to be prepared at the United Nations, sometimes even years.

Ustinov, the Russian, was obviously attempting to tamper with the personnel director's responsibility to write an official contract for me. Perhaps I could be intimidated and perhaps I would go back to my old job in the U.S. government.

I told the director that I was sure my contract was going to set a record for promptness and immunity from obstruction.

"Well . . . in your case . . . the papers in your dossier are . . . not complete," he revealed with considerable hesitation.

"How is that? It wasn't much, I must admit, but I filled out everything I was sent."

"We do not have your marriage license, Monsieur Sanjuan, and your religious affiliation has been left blank. Are you Christian or Jewish?"

"I was married in England, believe it or not, at St. Margaret's, part of Westminster Abbey. Our license, issued by the archbishop of Canterbury, is a large, medieval parchment without punctuation, but it bears a

lovely seal. It is framed and hangs in our bedroom, and I have no intention of bringing it here. Do you suppose that I could have spent twenty-
seven years in the U.S. government and successfully endured multiple
security clearances without being legally married to someone I claim as
my wife? As for my religion, I never fill that in on any form. It is none
of your business!"

"It is not you the United Nations has doubts about. It is those
Arabs, you know. They claim to have wives and dependents but they al-
most always lie," confided the director. "But if you are Jewish . . . or
Christian, of course . . . you would have only one wife, wouldn't you?"

"Well," I replied, "I don't believe any of that piffle. Arabs, for some
of whom I have great respect and affection, don't lie any more than the
British or the French or the people of Niger." The personnel director
was from Niger. "So you better find some other outrageous excuse for
stonewalling."

"Have you a receipt for payment for the marriage license?" he inquired, somewhat sheepishly.

"How do I know? It cost a lot of money, but I don't know about the
receipt—if there was any or where it is."

That night my wife and I looked through our scrapbooks and finally
found something that looked much like an ordinary laundry bill. It was
for seventy-five pounds, however, and we figured it could have been the
receipt for paying the marriage license fee.

I gave the unimpressive piece of paper to the personnel director
the next day. He nodded and, lo and behold, handed me my contract,
all neatly prepared with a duplicate! I signed the original and kept the
copy.

A few days later Undersecretary-General Ustinov smiled, this time
most inappropriately, and said to me, "I see you sign contract."

"What contract?" I replied. "Yes, I guess I did. I really don't remember."

But the Soviet UN mafia would not give up on me. After all, I was
a possible Jew, who was, most definitely, a dependable American. Obviously I was not ordinary UN material.

CHAPTER FOUR

The Soviet Mafia at Work

ithin a few months of my arrival, I found out what most people in the Secretariat already knew, that the Soviets were using the UN principally as a disguised but well-staffed intelligence collection agency. Among the most knowledgeable insiders was Javier Pérez de Cuellar himself. The secretary-general joked frequently about Soviet control of certain "critical" sectors in the Secretariat. The ubiquitous control of all that the Soviets deemed useful had endless anecdotal possibilities, of which cynical souls in the Secretariat made frequent use to lighten the daily boredom that otherwise prevailed in the UN ivory tower. The main theme of this kind of idle banter was that the Soviets did all sorts of outrageous things right in New York City under the noses of the gullible Americans. Everybody considered this American ingenuousness especially amusing simply because it was "so" American.

The Soviets had in place an extremely well-organized yet amazingly simple system of overt intelligence collection. As a result of an unbelievably informal arrangement of long standing with the United States, the Soviets totally controlled the well-staffed UN Secretariat library. Another part of the Secretariat, the Russian translation division, the largest foreign language team in the Secretariat, was rarely available to produce ordinary, run-of-the-mill translations, even for the secretary-general himself.

The memorandum is the preferred form of communication at the UN, where "notes," "papers," "studies," and "homilies" are scarce, lacking the gravity imparted by the tetrasyllabic Latin noun.

It is by means of such weighty documents written in an English dialect known as "UN-ese" that profound thoughts like the following are communicated back and forth:

"However, notwithstanding the importance of the issue, it, nevertheless, could be noted that, should the Security Council make a decision to evaluate the damage inflicted on Iraq, it may wish to adopt a resolution specifying a mandate of the Secretary-General thereto."

At one point I was making a reference (in a memorandum) to former undersecretary-general for political and Security Council affairs (there are no acronyms for UN titles, alas!) Arkady Shevchenko, the infamous (at the UN) Soviet defector. Thus I needed to refer to a copy of his then best-selling book *Breaking with Moscow.*

"Ellen," I said on the intercom to one of my secretaries. She entered my office with more alacrity than most other members of my staff could muster, which was why I had selected her for the delicate mission of going to the UN library to get me the book.

"You want that book!" she exclaimed, and I nodded assent.

An hour and a half later Ellen reappeared, bookless.

"They say they are busy and that, moreover, they don't have the book because it is a 'bad' book. I took so long because I had to wait an age until one of those creeps finally paid attention to me."

"Follow me!" I commanded, and in a short while we were both passing the circulation desk of the Dag Hammarskjöld Library. I led her to the card catalog.

"You won't find it there. I already looked," Ellen volunteered.

"*Mein Kampf*?" I asked. "Oh, I think they may have that. Yes, here it is in the catalog, by Adolf Hitler, no less." Ellen looked puzzled.

"But," she began and got no further, for I led her by the wrist to the circulation desk.

Three male individuals behind the counter studiously avoided my pleas to be excused and the right index finger I was waving in the air. Obviously aware of my polite demand for attention, they were nevertheless still avoiding my undeniable presence in front of them.

"HEY!" I shouted next, not only triggering their involuntary startle reflexes, but drawing glares from other people milling about.

"We are busy!" exclaimed the tallest of the three, with a very palpable Russian accent.

"Nowhere near as busy as you are going to be if you continue to ignore us!"

"What is it?" the Russian mouthpiece replied.

"Vy ochen bezmaniernyi," or "You are very rude," I said in Russian.

That changed the status of the negotiations. All the noise I was making probably had forced the tall Russian to wonder who I was. Was I one of them, one of us, one of whom? He stepped forward, still profoundly annoyed.

"I want you to get me a copy of Arkady Shevchenko's *Breaking with Moscow.* The secretary-general wants it. If you don't produce it within what I would consider a reasonable span of time, then you may perhaps want to explain, in the secretary-general's own office, why you are too busy to run this place like a library."

"Look," said the now slightly apprehensive Russian librarian, "that book is not in library because we don't have it in library because it is bad book. I can't give you what we don't have in library. Please excuse."

I looked derisively at this fellow, now flanked by his cohorts, who had stepped forward in a gesture of solidarity. "I have just looked up *Mein Kampf,* by Adolf Hitler, in your card catalog," I said. "That is generally regarded as a bad book. A very bad book. But you do have it—for use as a reference source, I imagine. Surely Shevchenko's benign opus couldn't be that bad. You know what I'm talking about?"

"I don't know Mein Whatever. I don't know that book!" the Russian librarian said, turning around, trying to disengage.

"You've heard of Adolf Hitler, haven't you? Also spelled H-Ü-T-L-E-R, whose mother was a Schickelgruber, I believe. You know about him, don't you?" I said, again raising my voice and causing a disturbance.

"Yes, I knew Hitler. I knew him!" the pseudo-librarian said.

"That's funny," I retorted, "you don't look old enough to have known Hitler!"

"Didn't you want that Hitler book?" Ellen inquired as we headed in defeat back to our office.

"No, thanks, I've read it already!" I said.

The UN library, of course, was essentially a front. Sure, they had books, periodicals, documents, and so on. They also had, as I gradually found out, a bloated library staff overwhelmingly composed of Soviet library "experts" who did everything their government required them to do except run a conventional library.

The director of the library—by a formal arrangement long predating my arrival—was always a Soviet official selected by the Soviet government. Why did the Soviets need monopolistic control of the UN library? They needed to be in charge not only because of the dubious Soviet specialty in libraries, but also because of their information collection activities, a rather well-developed science in different quarters of the Soviet government.

And why had the United States agreed to this absurd degree of Soviet control of the UN library? I tried to find out, but the consensus at the US-UN mission was that such a Soviet monopoly concerned only the UN library. What harm could that do? Just a library!

With a little more research, I was able to determine that the UN library under the monolithic management of the Soviets was probably the most comprehensive intelligence collection machine the USSR had in the United States. A river of information the width of the Amazon was flowing regularly to the UN library and from there to the UN Russian translation division, staffed totally by Soviet-seconded translators.

No wonder the UN "librarians" were too busy to find books for the secretary-general. And no wonder Arkady Shevchenko's book rated higher on the UN index *librorum prohibitorum* than *Mein Kampf,* by what's-his-name!

Always on behalf of the UN secretary-general, the UN Secretariat library targeted information, requested by intelligence agencies in Moscow, to be obtained from the Stanford Research Institute, from the Rand Corporation and other U.S. Department of Defense contractors, occasionally from the Advanced Research Projects Agency of the Department of Defense (believe it or not), and from multiple other valuable sources. In addition, of course, research information was obtained from congressional offices in Washington, American universities, companies, banks, stockbrokers, and a myriad more sources willing to supply the "UN" with facts and figures about anything the "UN" wanted. None of these sources would have honored a request from the Soviet embassy in Washington. Coming from the UN Secretariat, however, the requests were considered "legitimate," and the well-targeted information (not secret, but extremely useful and vast) was courteously and diligently sent to the UN library. Many of the sources must have even felt honored to be asked for such valuable information by the UN.

The scope of the material gathered at the UN in New York for Soviet intelligence use cannot be classified easily under any particular category. It was whatever the different Soviet users requested, and it covered a vast array of constantly changing topics. Under clever subterfuges the Soviet agents at the UN library would request a defense contractor for the firing sequence of U.S. intercontinental ballistic missiles in case of a nuclear exchange between the U.S. and the USSR, claiming that the UN secretary-general needed the data used in war-gaming scenarios in order to better focus UN studies on conflict resolution.

An American car manufacturer would be asked to submit unclassified but abundant material on the specifications of U.S. main battle tanks to help refine the UN's disarmament proposals in Geneva. Constant requests went forth for the names of officials in the U.S. government, or in changing congressional staffs in key committees like Foreign Affairs or military appropriations. Frequent requests for information on national and state parks and rural areas constantly updated Soviet targeting grids on the U.S.

Once the practice was established of asking for data on a myriad of intelligence-related subjects, the UN was known over the years as a very thorough and inquisitive information-collecting international organization, just as legitimate as numerous Swedish disarmament-promoting agencies or the Swiss Red Cross. There was nothing unusual about these UN activities, except that the UN was not actually meaningfully involved in bilateral disarmament negotiations between the U.S. and the USSR. For the private agencies overseas promoting arms control, this was in many cases their sole reason for existing.

Not only did the UN library collect for Soviet intelligence use information on U.S. military strategy and equipment; it also maintained an accurate record of the large, extended U.S. defense establishment, including its contractors and defense-funded researchers in American colleges and universities.

I acquired an increasingly comprehensive picture of the scope of Soviet UN library–related intelligence collection activities from veteran members of my staff, some of them gradually disaffected Soviets, Poles, Romanians, and other Iron Curtain–sponsored UN employees, and from officials of East European missions. As the decay in the Soviet Union became more apparent, these individuals tried, by confiding in me, to establish a bond with the top American "spy," which might come in handy in order to guarantee a more permanent resident status for themselves in the U.S.

From the UN Secretariat library the information was passed on in bulk to the Russian translation division at the UN Secretariat. There, it was sorted out by seconded Soviet analysts and translated. The most important items in what was literally a sea of material were sent to the Soviet UN mission in New York, and from there, via inviolate diplomatic pouches, to the Soviet Ministry of Foreign Affairs, the Soviet Ministry of External Economic Relations, the KGB, and various military intelligence outfits.

Overt intelligence in large quantities has always been much more valuable to the Soviets than stolen "secrets." Material obtained from published documents and periodicals was the basis, for example, for replicating state-of-the-art U.S. military aircraft, many of whose details, particularly relating to aerodynamics and aircraft design, have always been available, even in technical publications through which U.S. equipment is sold on the international arms market. Why does the MiG-29 look like a copy of the F-14? Because it is.

Having mapped out rather early in my stay at the UN the simple but effective infrastructure of the UN Secretariat Soviet intelligence-gathering operation, I informed Jeane Kirkpatrick, the American UN ambassador, who said she was astonished. She passed my succinct report on to the U.S. State Department and was told that State knew all about it, but had decided not to make an issue of it since that would "destabilize" our relationships at the UN and might even require asking Soviet staff members to leave the U.S. Indeed it might! The State Department added that it did not wish to expose U.S. diplomats in Moscow to retaliation. That was another specious excuse for doing nothing.

Of course, other options remained available to the Department of State. For example, it could have notified U.S. government offices that the UN library was under Soviet control and requested that no information, overt or otherwise, be provided to the UN. The State Department reply could have been predicted even before I ventured that suggestion.

To send around such a heads-up in Washington, I was told, would have disturbed our stable relations with the UN. That was an outcome the Department of State found undesirable. One might therefore say that the Department of State was fully supportive of the Soviet intelligence-gathering operations in the UN Secretariat. To be absolutely fair, the Soviet Foreign Ministry tried to reciprocate this American courtesy, but only by allowing the American embassy in Moscow to stay in the center of town, thus permitting American diplomats to look out the embassy windows whenever there were Red Army parades.

Since all this hocus-pocus appeared to be well known to everybody, including the UN building guards, and perhaps to the cleaning crews as well, I became interested in the degree of Soviet control of other Secretariat activities. By the time I had been in the place for a year, I had unearthed many more curious facts about Soviet bureaucratic hegemony at the UN.

Soviet control was not restricted to the Secretariat library and the extensive Russian translation facilities. The Soviets actually controlled every important aspect of the UN Secretariat. Soviet UN officials occupied many pivotal posts. These were not necessarily top positions, but extremely useful ones, nevertheless.

For example, in the area of personnel, eventually renamed Department of Human Resources, the Soviets always controlled strategic jobs of which they never let go. It is redundant to repeat that these shenanigans were well known, particularly to all those officials who staffed the personnel department, and certainly to the present UN secretary-general, Kofi Annan, while he occupied the position of director of personnel. The accepted and prevalent view was that if the Soviets chose to pervert the UN system and the Americans chose to let them, it certainly was no skin off anybody else's nose.

In the Department of Public Information, it was the same story. In the Department of Political and Security Council Affairs, the Soviets manipulated all the top and second-echelon positions, crucial in running that department. And so forth throughout the UN Secretariat, the Soviets being able thus to steer by means of Soviet-seconded officials, or surrogates from other Soviet bloc countries and subservient nations, the practical day-to-day running of the Secretariat.

Here I should briefly explain the unique staffing practices of the UN Secretariat. The Secretariat consists of staffs that come from the different member states in rough proportion to the percentage of the assessed budget these states are supposed to contribute to the UN. The big exceptions to this arrangement are the United States and Israel.

The United States has always been officially assessed between one-third and one-quarter of the total budget. However, taking into account all U.S. monetary contributions, voluntary and otherwise, U.S. tax exemptions granted to the UN, and other contributions that are made "in kind"—that is, in services—the U.S. contributes much more than that. In fact, since other UN member states have often made contributions in soft money rather than in hard currency, the U.S. has been and still is the overwhelming and totally indispensable underwriter of the UN.

If the U.S. were to insist on being allocated a proportion of the staff commensurate with its massive share of funding, there would be a hugely disproportionate majority of Americans in the Secretariat, and the U.S. would be accused of dominating the place. So the number of U.S. professionals has been limited to just over four hundred, give or take a few.

But American professionals in the UN Secretariat are recruited off the street, so to speak. Americans are rarely endorsed by the U.S. government, nor do the overwhelming majority of them feel they owe anything like allegiance to the United States. They feel they are true and responsible international civil servants who owe their allegiance to the UN and its lofty, if sometimes rusty, principles.

That would be all well and good if the other members of the Secretariat staff also felt and acted like model international civil servants. But during the entire fifty-year Cold War period, all Secretariat staff members from the USSR and the Eastern European Soviet bloc countries, as well as from China and a number of other member states, have served on what is called "secondment," as has been outlined before. That translates into their being agents under the sponsorship of the governments of their countries of origin.

In addition to that "well-balanced" system of secondment, countries not officially seconding their nationals have also jealously protected their UN staff member nationals working in the Secretariat. With the exception of the Americans, all other UN Secretariat staff members are supported and fought for by their governments, if for no other reason than to protect the influence of those member states within the Secretariat, where member states are not supposed to have any influence.

So most nonseconded, "regular" staff members are, to a significant degree, also agents of their governments in the Secretariat. That includes the French, the British, the Germans, the Spanish, the Brazilians, and so on—as well as all the Middle Easterners, of course.

And the Israelis?

Until relatively recently, no Israelis needed to apply, for none were hired by the UN Secretariat, and extremely few American Jews were inducted, either. That iniquity toward Israel has marginally changed, but the Israeli UN quota has been filled with a fair number of Israeli Palestinians in order to continue to keep authentic Israeli Jews to a minimum.

Positions in the UN Secretariat become open periodically. But Soviet-seconded UN Secretariat staff members stayed at the UN for about two years or worked on a temporary, three-month renewable contract basis. How then did the Soviets manage to maintain constant control of so many bureaucratic fulcrums in the Secretariat?

The Soviet arrangement was ingenious, although it had depended on the mind-boggling stupidity of the U.S. mission to the UN and the subliminal shortstopping functions of the U.S. Department of State.

The Soviet arrangement worked like this. Small Third World member states had small representations in the UN Secretariat. In many cases these small states were five or ten people below their quota within the overall Secretariat staff. Such small representations could be easily wiped out by sickness, death, or retirement. When these countries lost by attrition a significant post, it would frequently be filled by an official from another country, and soon the little countries would not have even minimal influence in the Secretariat.

Never mind that positions were not supposed to be allocated in response to member states' desires to have influence in the Secretariat. That argument had long been made moot by Soviet KGB infiltration by means of the system of Soviet secondment. Nevertheless, the Soviets proposed to the UN General Assembly that an "underrepresented" member state should be able to keep vacated positions in the UN Secretariat that would be reserved for replacements from that same state until the proper quota level had been reached or surpassed by that state.

The United States mission and the Department of Nice (i.e., State) quickly signed on to the Soviet-proposed General Assembly resolution codifying this very "equitable" system. Of course, the Americans were also friends of the Third World! The resolution passed by consensus or unanimously, a heartwarming example of cooperation between the superpowers.

From that point forward, the Soviet Union consistently fell slightly behind in appointing seconded officials to the Secretariat, and thus the USSR itself became a chronically underrepresented member state. In lieu of making permanent (two-year) appointments exclusively, the Soviet Union now made a fairly large number of three-month temporary appointments that did not count as part of the Soviet quota and were renewable indefinitely. Thus, the Soviets maintained their contingent of agents undiminished. The bonus was that all positions occupied until that point by Soviet-seconded officials would now be reserved exclusively for Soviet replacements, since the Soviet Union, even with a large staff, was also officially underrepresented. And any new positions the Soviets could infiltrate would thenceforth be permanently reserved for Soviet replacements.

Meanwhile, the vetting of any Americans being considered for employment was thorough to the point of excess. Files up to six inches thick were compiled on each applicant and reviewed with painstaking care, ostensibly to make sure that no bad apples snuck through, or even little bad cherries. Such careful scrutiny was in fact an effort to find political pretexts to deny American applications. Regular American professionals were considered only if they could prove they had no contact with the U.S. government. With their virtual control of the UN personnel system, the Soviets made sure that American agents were not introduced into the Secretariat to match the Soviet-seconded staff at the middle and lower professional levels.

Naturally, at the highest levels, American political appointees were occasionally accepted for reasons of sensible expediency. In spite of the fact that there was no nonsuicidal way to deny Vice President George Bush's demand to Javier Pérez de Cuellar that I be appointed, nevertheless the dossier compiled on me was also more than six inches thick. Rather than a profile, it contained a layer-by-layer sonogram of my real as well as my fictitious identity.

But American applicants for middle and lower-level positions who had any prior U.S. political connections were repeatedly rejected.

Senator John Warner of Virginia, with whom I had worked in

Washington when he was secretary of the navy, asked me to interview a young woman from his staff who had an excellent international affairs background and was genuinely interested in working at the UN. I recommended that she be accepted as an applicant, and I got the U.S. mission to support her application. Our support was the kiss of death. After six months of haggling about her application, it was not even accepted for consideration, and Warner was furious. I mentioned this to the secretary-general, but he had no idea who Senator Warner was. During the ten years I spent at the Secretariat, it became quite obvious to me that nationals of any country who did not have the support of their mission at the UN would not be considered for employment—except for Americans. For them it was the opposite. With the support of their government, Americans would be automatically disqualified.

Soviet and Soviet bloc candidates on the other hand were virtually sight-unseen acceptances. All that was required was a skimpy two-page application listing name, address, education, and desired UN position, presented by their government in a prearranged procedure that did not actually involve real UN approval. Any Russian, however, not formally approved by the Soviet government would be automatically disqualified.

What a deal!

I shall describe two representative cases.

Valery Zdorovenin worked in my division and was supposed to be an expert on maritime issues, particularly the Law of the Sea, concerning which there had been no movement at the UN for more than fifteen years. He was supposed to be an oceanographer who had traveled extensively around the world with Soviet fishing fleets. It was quite obvious that the extent of his oceanographic duties on these ships had been to perform the espionage activities that all Soviet fishing fleets, with their large factory ships, conducted a few miles offshore, just outside the territorial waters of the United States and NATO countries and near many other sensitive parts of the world.

Zdorovenin was quite a nice fellow, with an infectious Russian sense of humor and a certain personal disposition to confess. My first meaningful contact with him was when I asked him one day to stay a little bit after 5:00 P.M. to go over a report he had produced. "I can't do that," he said.

"Why can't you do that, may I ask? I know you people scramble out of here before five o'clock, but I must insist that today you stay," I said with a frown. I remember the frown very well.

"No, Mr. Sanjuan, I can't stay, for I must catch the bus back to our quarters in Riverdale, you know," he replied like a schoolboy facing the principal.

"Well, catch another bus, for God's sake! Or take the subway!" I replied, my frown now more deeply embossed on my forehead.

"Mister Sanjuan, you don't understand," Zdorovenin said, almost wailing. "It is Soviet bus to Riverdale, our compound, where we live. They take attendance at the bus and, if I'm not there, I'm in deep shit, as you say here."

"So, how do you go downtown to the theater or for dinner or to the movies?" I asked, not quite swallowing his story yet.

"We don't usually go to those places, but if we have to go somewhere, it has to be with official approval, like to get a pair of shoes or buy a new boom box. You know we love the boom boxes. We don't have any in Russia," Zdorovenin disarmingly explained.

"Go get your damn bus!" I told him. I realized that these poor people were virtual prisoners in New York.

A few years later, Zdorovenin had become as much of a friend of mine as his peculiar circumstances would permit. Finally one day, I took him to lunch in Chinatown at 20 Mott Street, my favorite cheap authentic Hunan emporium. He had never been to Chinatown after all his time in the Big Apple.

As we were eating stuffed oysters, he began to tell me stories of his life. He finally confessed that on one of his fishing expeditions, he had clandestinely purchased a large quantity of cheap dolls somewhere in the Orient in order to smuggle them into Russia and sell them at a good profit, for such foreign toys were much in demand then in the

USSR. As soon as he stepped off the ship in Vladivostok, the KGB border police arrested him and searched the ship for the boxes of dolls. That, he said, was his last fishing trip. As punishment he was sent to the UN.

So the Soviets were sending to the UN Secretariat convicted smugglers whom they could control all the more effectively. Their criminal standing in no way impeded their being accepted, for the UN did not need any information that went much beyond name, rank, and serial number. An overdose of speeding tickets, on the other hand, or a recommendation from Senator Warner disqualified any hapless, well-qualified American seeking to make a career out of the UN.

Poor Zdorovenin finally came to me one day in dire straits. He had met an American during lunchtime at a bar on Second Avenue who had identified himself as being with "the U.S. federal secret police," and who had suggested that he leave the UN and go to Washington to reveal Soviet secrets. What should he do, he asked—me of all people!

I told poor, hapless Zdorovenin that I could not do a great deal for him, but that I doubted that anyone would identify himself as being with "the U.S. federal secret police."

"Oh, yes, yes, Mr. Sanjuan, that's exactly what fellow said!" Zdorovenin protested.

My friends in the bureau told me that my Russian staff member must be delirious, and I decided to stay clear of whatever imbroglio Zdorovenin had become involved in.

"Well then, I am going to protest to Soviet mission that your government is tampering with a UN official," Zdorovenin foolishly proclaimed.

"It's your Soviet mission," I said.

Several days later I began to miss Zdorovenin in the office. My secretary told me that he had left in a hurry a few days before, saying that he was not coming back.

While looking at the flashing numbers above the UN elevator door, I caught peripheral sight of Vassily Safronchuk, the Soviet undersecretary-general who had succeeded Ustinov. "What happened to our friend

Zdorovenin?" I asked him, even though in UN elevators people normally avoided conversations.

Safronchuk lifted both eyebrows and gave forth with an enigmatic smile. Once out of the steel cage, he turned to me and said, "Yes, well, Valery Zdorovenin became sick. He has chronic disease that only in Soviet Union can be treated. We have very good doctors and hospitals in Soviet Union, as you know."

Zdorovenin's successor was a certain Victor Tsarev, another "expert" on the chronically dormant Law of the Sea. He presented himself in my office with a little piece of paper that contained a very short biography, which he gave me along with a ten-page study he had presumably written on the law of the briny deep. The paper was in French because French was the proper language at the UN—as he pointed out to me in Russian.

"Alors, vous connaissez la langue de Racine!" I exclaimed in French.

"Nyet. Tol'ko chitaioo. Ne govorioo," he replied. "I only read it. I do not speak it," indicating that he at least suspected that what I had just said to him was in French.

It turned out that Tsarev, having presented his credentials-conveying paper in French, had thereby fulfilled his professional requirements in advance. He thereafter confined himself to coming in at 10:00 A.M. and soon to disappearing for the rest of the day, unless he occasionally reappeared at lunchtime, but only in order to further authenticate his presence.

One day, going to lunch again to my favorite Mott Street eatery with a few other members of my staff, including two Russian-speaking Poles (one the former member of the Communist Party Central Committee in Warsaw), I caught Tsarev at the door. "Come with us to lunch in Chinatown," I said to him, which he misunderstood to be an order.

At lunch Tsarev said nothing at all until I encouraged him to break the ice, pointing to the encyclopedic menu and intruding on his silence with "Chinese food is the best ever. I highly recommend the stuffed oysters."

Tsarev had the stuffed bivalves, making a wry face while declaring them very tasty, "Ochen' vkusno!" He then remained quiet for a long time. Finally he ventured in halting English, "In Moscow we also have excellent Chinese restaurant."

"In New York," I shamelessly replied, "we have 60,325 Chinese restaurants."

"Oh, yes, where?" Tsarev inquired.

"Look around you as we leave. There are 450 of them right here on Mott Street!"

Tsarev's charm consisted of his obvious incompetence. Maybe he was good at encoding secret messages that were sent back to Moscow. Had he been a lowly American, he never would have passed muster to enter the UN.

The Soviets were very clever not to give the impression of going after all the top posts in the Secretariat, but they went for pivotal number two and three posts in all departments that were not already conceded as Soviet territory. The Department of Political and Security Council Affairs, the UN Secretariat library, and the Russian translation division were unofficially conceded as total Soviet jurisdictions.

In the personnel department the Soviets maintained especially tight control. Through their well-placed agents in "permanent" posts, they could keep track of all private matters relating to the lives of non-Soviet staff members, giving them particularly useful information for contract renewal time. Madame Boyer in the sovietized political and Security Council affairs department superintended their work.

At crucial junctures in any UN staff member's career, the Soviets knew what medical debts the particular individual had, what mortgages, what outstanding bank loans—in other words, the degree of comfort or desperation the contract-holder lived under, and to what extent a contract renewal could be used to coerce this person into occasional collaboration.

How could the U.S. government be tricked into tolerating such an abuse of power? In fact, it was easy to understand the why and wherefore of this American tolerance. Once the Soviet "underrepresentation" stratagem became obvious, there was no way to reverse it, for that would have put the U.S. in a position of curtailing the rights and hard-won privileges of the little underrepresented countries as well as the hard-won but outrageous privileges of the deliberately underrepresented Soviets.

By 1986, all these sly shenanigans and underhanded maneuvers had become totally obvious to me, as they were to every member of the UN Secretariat who had a slightly above average IQ. During trips to Washington to see congressmen and senators or their staffs, I tried to point out the degree of control the Soviets had attained and would continue to develop in the UN Secretariat. The legislators I visited were of my own choosing, for Javier Pérez de Cuellar did not have any grasp of—nor did he care about—what was going on in the U.S. Congress. He figured the Department of State would take care of getting the money out of Congress for him, and he was right. His interest in wooing the solons in Washington was more personal. He liked to hobnob with powerful political figures even if he could not tell a Democrat from a Republican. Therefore, I had carte blanche.

With a few exceptions—Senator Hatch, Senator Kassebaum, Senator Hollings, Senator D'Amato, Representative Scheuer, and a very few others—Congress considered the UN a waste of time and something Americans funded just to keep the Third World happy.

Still, the Soviet maneuvers and deceptions—and particularly their brazen intelligence collection activities—bothered me plenty. At a luncheon with Pérez de Cuellar, I mentioned to him in passing that, in the long run, news of these outrageous abuses would hit the fan, and the American public might well pressure Congress to strangle the UN financially.

"Well, Don Pedro," he said, "if either the U.S. mission or you personally can bring to me a fully documented case of Soviet espionage in the Secretariat, I will proceed without hesitation to have that individual removed from this building and sent back to Russia!"

I smiled. He knew damn well that no such case could be "documented," given the inaccessibility of the sacrosanct UN premises to U.S.

investigators. He also knew that although I had a great deal of information—almost as much as he—I was not in a position to build a case-by-case, action-by-action, document-by-document "dossier" on anyone.

On the issue of Soviet control, UN secretaries-general were not stupid, uninformed, or even complicit. They were none of these things in view of the lack of concern for its own interests evinced by the U.S. government.

In 1988 my first five-year term expired, and like any other UN official—including the secretary-general—I was up for renewal. That renewal was normally considered automatic. But, in a moment of idle banter at another luncheon, Ustinov, then still Soviet undersecretary-general, with a sly look, asked me if I was planning to stay around. He related that disingenuous question to the size of my mortgage, implying that he knew exactly how much I owed since the Sovs knew everything about everyone.

This information almost certainly came from my income tax returns. As an American UN official, I was required to present my returns to the UN so that it could transfer them to the U.S. Treasury Department and get approval for my UN staff contribution, which was the equivalent of my U.S. income tax. All that private information as well as a number of other personal items—for I was compelled by Treasury to claim all the exemptions any American was entitled to in filling out the return—were available, through a Soviet stooge in personnel working for Kofi Annan, to the top Soviet staff member and his KGB control officer or perhaps to Madame Boyer.

Addressing Ustinov's impertinent questions, I said, "Please do not take too much offense at my reply to your query, but there is a Russian expression I would like to substitute in lieu of a more specific answer." I used a very strong expletive with reference to the Soviet undersecretary-general's mother, a common practice in Russia referred to as *materit*.

My Russian colleague left the lunch, perhaps to avoid apoplexy, and returned only when dessert was being served. There were no repercussions.

CHAPTER FIVE

How the KGB Controlled the Secretariat

I have long enjoyed polite professional relations with bona fide members of the KGB. Therefore, although I do not pretend to have detailed knowledge of past worldwide KGB or current Russian intelligence operations, I have had considerable involvement with a rather unique range of Soviet undercover activities. For these chummy dealings with the "enemy," I have not been arrested, court-martialed, declared an enemy combatant, or branded a traitor. On the contrary, I have been given a commendation from the Federal Bureau of Investigation, which I proudly display on my office wall. Go figure!

As the reader may have noticed, a confluence of bizarre circumstances long ago created a paradoxical UN environment immune from external oversight, but within which very little could be kept confidential. Indeed, there was no need for the Soviets and other foreign operatives to maintain too much security inside the Secretariat, since it was and remains a closed society, a remarkably cozy brotherhood for a significant number of "international civil servants" sometimes engaged in subterfuge and crime—confederates as well as antagonists rubbing shoulders with each other in rather close quarters.

I knew what they were about. They knew what I was about. I told the

FBI, but the FBI could do very little about the information I provided. The Department of State did not want to know. Meanwhile, the Soviet operatives could do very little to thwart my snooping because it was not to their benefit to create a scene by trying to get rid of me.

To understand all this better, it may be useful to note that the final architectural plan of the UN Secretariat building had an ominous beginning. It was based on a design by the French architect Le Corbusier, who conceived of buildings as sculpture, not necessarily inhabitable. His design would have placed the whole forty-story UN skyscraper slab on *pilotis*—a massive array of columns. This regardless of the arctic winds that sweep up and down the East River estuary in winter in New York. UN officials would have faced terrible discomfort while waiting for the elevators had the *pilotis* idea survived.

Le Corbusier eventually quit, saying that the building was being designed by "a committee," and a modified UN Secretariat building was indeed designed by a committee. It is a most impractical structure, with narrow but long corridors and very limited office space on each floor. The slablike design consists of superimposed slivers of space. Each floor is divided in two by six elevator shafts and a generously proportioned women's restroom. Further up the hall, each floor is truncated again by a generous men's restroom and a forty-story shaft separating the Secretariat building from an independent, massive concrete internal fire escape that resembles an endless grand staircase. Another grand staircase also takes up space on all floors on the other side of the elevators.

In short, the UN Secretariat is hell for those who suffer from rheumatoid arthritis and a paradise for those with poor bladder control, offering as it does approximately one hundred restrooms for both sexes.

The building nevertheless provides a random element of communal intimacy since its impractical layout requires that all of the Secretariat's many departments be dispersed among several floors. As we have already seen, the functions of the varied UN Secretariat departments are confusing and seem to be repeatedly duplicated in each department. There is very little cooperation among departments. That is not too hard to understand since the duplicative functions make all departments virtually self-sufficient—like medieval duchies under a powerless monarch—and the lack of identifiable substance makes most departments appear superfluous, and therefore they easily function independently of each other.

To compound the chaos of commingling the staffs of departments that jealously avoid sharing their duplicative functions, there is the altitude prestige factor. The upper floors of the building are highly esteemed real estate. Once departments were established and had seized possession of segments of the upper floors, their subsequent growth was accommodated in the middle and lower floors, sort of helter-skelter. Such glorious, organically grown confusion now makes everybody run into everybody else and, thus, everyone easily notes who sees whom and why.

In the late 1980s, as the hegemony of the USSR began to show unmistakable cracks and approached terminal collapse, the UN KGB types began to face up to the prospect of collective orphanhood. Naturally enough, they preferred to stay as long as possible in the land of plenty. And who was the American they knew best, had most frequent contact with, and, paradoxically, trusted the most? Why, me, of course, the American spy whom they saw and talked to every day.

They constantly sought my advice. They asked for assistance in procuring pro bono legal services when they or their wives were involved in traffic accidents, or received threatening calls from New York Russian mafia extortionists, or wanted to tell their stories to the press or to university audiences. They feasted me finally in Moscow at the best Soviet restaurant, the Praga—probably the principal reason why McDonald's became a luxury emporium after 1992.

Who, as a class, were these KGB and other Soviet gumshoe characters?

As a group they were a rather intelligent and sophisticated bunch. They had a subtle appreciation of the human predicament and, accompanying that, a refined Russian sense of humor.

In the USSR, with all its boils and carbuncles, the American saying "military intelligence is an oxymoron" did not really apply. In an authoritarian society, the best people tended to gravitate to the most authoritarian professions—most notably the secret police in any of its many manifestations. The KGB was a huge operation, not all of it involved in espionage by any means. It had an army that protected the Soviet frontiers, ran overt and covert operations, and made it the KGB's business to mind everybody else's business. Many of the USSR's best and brightest went into the KGB.

The UN Secretariat in New York was a preferred KGB assignment. The KGB types could relax there, play hide-and-seek with their American "adversaries," and afford themselves the luxury of sampling the sweet gifts of decadent capitalism.

"Pedro, plis do me favor," a certain Kharitonov asked me one day. "Look at camera I just bought at Central Camera in Central Grand."

"Grand Central," I corrected him. To speak to me in Russian was a compliment the UN Russians frequently paid me. For me to speak to them in Russian too often would have been an insult meaning "Your English is not good enough."

"How much did you pay?" I asked.

"Three hundred and fifty dollars. It is Oyimpus. Very good," said Kharitonov, suspecting foul play.

"You got taken. You should have gotten it for $150," I pointed out with a heavy heart, but hoping to teach the KGB how to shop in our country.

"But is price list," he protested weakly.

"You never pay list price at Central Camera," I explained. "You ask 'How much?' The salesman tells you '$350.' You say 'I don't have much time for jokes, so now how much?' He says 'I can give it to you for $290. Are you at the UN? Then we have a special price of $250.' You turn around and say, 'Good-bye!' He says, 'Wait a minute, let me talk to the manager.' He quickly returns and says '$160 is the best we can do.' You say '$150, okay?' And you get the Olympus for less than half of the fairy-tale list price. That's the way to do it."

"But that like bazaar in Damascus. Not serious. In Soviet Union one price and you pay," Kharitonov whimpered.

"In Soviet Union, my friend, you can't buy an Olympus camera!" I retorted.

We both laughed.

But the laugh was really on me, for after that initial session on the virtues of capitalism, I had at least one friendly Soviet staff member come to my office each week to discuss how much to pay for a camera, binoculars, a telescope, or whatever else they had at Central Camera.

If my anecdote about Kharitonov appears condescending in tone, consider that in Moscow I did not have the foggiest idea what to pay for a camera, nor where to get one, nor that getting a camera, for me, a foreigner, was totally out of the question. On my second trip to Russia in the Soviet days, I found out that good cameras (they made some that weren't altogether bad) were available through the Ministry of Defense only after producing proof that you were a professional photographer— a member of the proper *profsoyus*—like the photographers' union.

Why the Ministry of Defense? Because optics had primarily military applications, so Defense was in charge.

Kharitonov and other KGB agents were quite open about their own *profsoyus* status—being professional KGB members, that is. While they never affirmed being with the KGB or GRU, they never denied it, either, and smiled broadly when I good-humoredly pointed an accusing finger at them. Naturally, all of them brought to the UN the minimal required credentials that assigned them to the Soviet Ministry of Foreign Affairs back home.

The most Dostoyevskian among these noble spies was the successor to Undersecretary-General Ustinov. Short and square, a blend of Scandinavian and Tartar antecedents with the telltale Russified Mongolian name of Vassily Sergeyevich Safronchuk, he was in his early sixties, displayed a healthy shock of white hair, and always sported a cagey smile that reflected a compounded inferiority complex.

There was nothing you could say or reveal that Safronchuk did not already know, including the blood pressure of a parakeet. "Ya uzhe znayoo!" "I already know that!" was the expression constantly on his lips.

A former artillery captain in the Red Army, he never failed to bring up the story of how his outfit had received a Studebaker truck during the war as lend-lease from the U.S., only to have it taken away by American forces retrieving U.S. property in Germany right after the war. The Yanks took the beloved Studebaker and blew it up a short distance away from Vassily and his men.

"Why did you do that? We loved our truck," he disconsolately but repeatedly complained, throwing the outrage in my face.

At first I commiserated with Safronchuk, but after hearing his sad story for the nth time, I told him that I had nothing to do with World War II, since it ended when I was barely a teenager, and that I really did not give a damn what had happened to their beloved Studebaker.

"Ya uzhe znayoo!" Vassily replied on cue.

But this overriding urge to know everything and then some was very useful to me, for I had a slightly different problem—I was curious. Our mutual, complementary psychological afflictions worked more to my advantage.

All one had to do to get Safronchuk to spill his beans was to explain to him anything that was inconsistent with facts that he thought he already possessed. Whenever the opportunity presented itself for Vassily to presume intellectual superiority—particularly vis-à-vis the American spy whom he blamed for the destruction of his beloved Studebaker—he would proudly hoist his colors and proceed to hold forth on the subject.

During numerous lunches at distant Spanish restaurants (among his foibles was a weakness for *angulas,* or small fried eels that cost a fortune in New York), I asserted that I understood how the KGB ran their operation in the UN Secretariat. What I told him was so preposterous and so full of ethnocentric American clichés that Vassily could not help but set me—and the CIA—straight. Vassily was convinced that I was a high-ranking CIA agent of brigadier general rank or above. That's a pretty high rank in the KGB. He intimated that such, indeed, was his own rank. And he knew how the CIA was organized, for he and his people knew all that very well "already."

Many invitations to eel-bearing restaurants (Fornos, Jai Alai, La Bilbaina, El Pote) did not cost me anything, for the FBI reimbursed me always in a parked, unmarked car at Forty-fourth Street and First Avenue, with two witnesses in the car, as FBI rules require.

Of course, the Soviet UN Secretariat staff members were not all KGB, Safronchuk explained. How could they be? The KGB role was managerial, so to speak. They ran the operation, if one could call it that—no differently from operations managed by UN Secretariat staff members from the People's Republic of China, or the French, or the British, or the Filipinos for that matter.

"What Filipinos are you talking about?" I exclaimed, pretending to be surprised.

"Filipinos control finance and staff assessment area of Department of Management. It is monopoly," Safronchuk confided. "Didn't you know? Only Americans are out of loop, as you say, at UN, except CIA has you, of course!"

I could not enlighten him to the contrary about being CIA, so I smiled enigmatically, Mona Lisa–style.

KGB types on the Secretariat staff were maybe thirty in number, the exact figure Vassily wouldn't say. The rest were specialists and reported to the managerial KGB staff, except for some Russians, very few, who were children of the *nomenklatura,* the powerful members of the Soviet Communist Party back home. These were untouchable and largely useless at the UN.

But again, Vassily explained during our tête-à-têtes, privileged appointments were common also among other national UN staff contingents—even the British, certainly the French, and all the Africans and Latin Americans. Vassily had a point.

Members of other countries that had what we Americans were fond of calling "communist" governments—Poles, Czechs, Hungarians, and so on—also had their own hierarchy, because state socialism was a system of government that was well organized, not incompetent as most capitalist governments tend to be. Vassily was a proud communist, and not without reason.

And because of the ideological affinity among all socialist governments, there was ample cooperation at the UN among their staffs. They all recognized their common bond. But did not the Brits and the Americans also feel a common bond? Again he had a point.

Vassily answered all his own questions, which for me was very convenient since I had to volunteer no embarrassing information in order
to keep the dialogue going—perhaps, about the disastrous lack of cohesion among American UN Secretariat staff members. In fact, it was
more of a monologue, with me playing the role of the attentive and
spellbound disciple.

The range of Safronchuk's boasting revelations confirmed—as if
such confirmation was necessary—that Soviet control among East European UN staffs was complete and that such control also involved the
staffs of many African countries from the sub-Saharan region. However,
he did consistently betray disdain for the North Africans and Middle
Easterners, the "Islamic bloc" as he called them, for they were lackeys of
the West.

All these "gems" of Dostoyevskian wisdom I assembled into coher-
ent, organized form and relayed to my contacts in Jim Fox's New York
FBI outfit, with not infrequent discussions with Fox himself at his favorite restaurant on Sixth Avenue. Jim and I would act very serious during the business portion of the meal, and would then allow ourselves a
laugh during the dessert, for we knew that neither the State Department
nor the CIA gave much of a damn about the KGB's activities at the UN.

During my periodic meetings with Vice President Bush in the
White House and in his office in the U.S. Senate, arranged by his affa-
ble assistant Jennifer Fitzgerald, I brought these concerns repeatedly to
his attention. The first such meeting occurred early in 1984.

I told Bush that Soviet intelligence collection was simple to describe
and an easy problem to deal with, provided the U.S. State Department decided to put a stop to it. On the other hand, the culture of anti-Semitism,
the cohesion among Islamic activists whom the U.S. State Department
then still regarded as friends of America, and the UN secretary-general's
sense of detachment from everything that was going on under his very nose
all constituted a much more complex problem, hard to grasp in all its ram-
ifications but even more urgent to resolve.

Bush asked me what I thought might be a way to deal with that
mess.

"Well, what I'm afraid of is that a widening chasm is developing between the UN and the U.S. Congress that is going to create increasingly difficult problems at the UN. The Soviets will not hesitate to pounce on this opportunity to use the disaffected elements at the UN to their advantage."

Already Senator Nancy Kassebaum was talking about introducing legislation to cut or withhold U.S. contributions to the UN because the UN wasted money.

"The wasting of money by the UN, which is hemorrhagic in character, is, nevertheless, the least of our worries," I told Bush. "All U.S. government departments and agencies waste tons of money, particularly if you look at government from the anarchist point of view that considers most government activities unnecessary. But the criminal, corrupt, clandestine, and conspiratorial goings-on in the UN Secretariat go much further beyond the pale and are potentially quite devastating. If the Congress becomes involved in investigating those—and I feel I ultimately have a duty to help clean up undertakings that hurt the U.S.—the break with the UN might be irreparable."

"So, what do you think can be done? I know the place all too well. I was U.S. permanent representative there myself."

"I know that, sir," I hastened to add. "What could be done is to bring the UN secretary-general to his senses about the dangers that lie ahead for him with the U.S. Congress."

"I know him, but not too well. Is he an articulate person?"

"In front of a large audience he is a crashing bore," I explained. "He reads his speeches as if they came out of the pages of the telephone directory. But before a small group, as in a seminar, he can be engaging, rather clever, sometimes even funny, and he can persuade and cajole those he talks to, and he also listens well."

"Perhaps we can get him to come to Washington to talk to a select group of senators so they can understand his problems and he can understand ours. Maybe I can give a dinner," Bush suggested.

"In the U.S. Senate?" I asked, thinking he would host it as president of the Senate.

"No, that's a bad idea," Bush said. "Uninvited senators have a way of popping in at those functions, and they can get out of control. No. At my house on Massachusetts Avenue [meaning the vice president's official residence] or at a club in Georgetown that I still belong to. What senators, though?"

"Well, senators like Percy and other Republican liberals are convinced internationalists, so they are a waste of time," I pointed out. "The extreme conservatives, on the other hand, are hopeless, for nothing can change their mind. Let's try, if you approve, the in-betweens who are reasonable people, like Hatch, Kassebaum of course, Kasten, Roth, Hollings, and so forth. I have talked to them, and they want reform at the UN that makes a difference."

Bush thought the category of in-betweens would be just right, for much could be done in the Senate with a few reasonable swing votes. With his blessing and a red, size-XXL sport shirt with his monogram that Bush gave out as a present, I set out to get agreement from Javier Pérez de Cuellar. Here was an excellent opportunity for this soft-spoken, somewhat timid secretary-general to show his stuff where it counted and for him to understand as well that the UN Secretariat was not going to be a battlefield much longer if things in Washington turned really nasty.

Don Javier received the proposal with lukewarm enthusiasm, mostly contrived, I thought. It was, however, a proposal from the vice president of the United States that a Peruvian who had social identity problems would respect and even fear not to accept.

"Let's do it after the first of the year [1985] or better by about the middle of March, when all the fuss over the General Assembly debate has died down."

"That sounds doable," I ventured, "although, naturally, we will have to take into account also the schedule of the vice president."

"And these senators, who are they?" Mr. Javier Pérez (for that was really his family name) inquired with a look of apprehension. I gave him the names Bush and I had discussed.

"That Jewish woman again. She hates us and is threatening to cut off our funds," Javier blurted.

I pretended to not understand. "What woman are you referring to, Don Javier?"

"The Kastenbaum [*sic*] senator. Her first name is Nancy or something."

"Senator Kassebaum is not Jewish. But I fail to see what difference it would make if she were. The more I look around in this Secretariat, the more I am appalled to perceive that being Jewish is regarded as a grievous character flaw, to put it mildly. When I first came here, that Soviet stooge Ustinov accused me of being Jewish and trapped me into a silly argument. Then I did the right thing and proudly proclaimed being Jewish."

"Oh, you are not Jewish," Don Javier said, waving his hand up and down. "We checked all that and we know."

"Well, Mr. Secretary-General," I told him somewhat angrily and altogether too flustered, "I may not be Jewish and may even know some Jewish people who don't like me, but I am regarded wherever I go, officially, as an enemy of racism and an opponent of anti-Semitism."

"Well, let's leave all that aside," Don Javier said, unaffected by my protest. "Let's have the Kastenbaum [*sic*] woman and the other senators at the dinner, too. I think the dinner probably is a good idea. You will be there with me, of course?"

"You can count on it!" I said.

Weeks passed, and Jenny Fitzgerald finally came up with a list of about fifteen senators handpicked by Bush. I verified with Don Javier Pérez that he had March 15 on his calendar as the agreed-upon date.

Later, as March approached, Jenny told me that the invitations had been sent to the Washington guests after checking with appropriate Senate staff members for the green light on March 15. The secretary-general would get his official invitation after the Senate replies were in, and we knew we had a dinner.

On March 1 enough acceptances had been received to guarantee a meaningful attendance, and I so informed the UN secretary-general.

"What dinner is this?" he asked, feigning disorientation.

"The dinner the vice president is holding at his residence for you to meet significant U.S. senators!"

"Had we settled on a date?" he asked disingenuously.

"Indeed we have, and, as you must remember, I personally verified it with you several times. The date, as a matter of fact, was of your own choosing. The invitations have all been sent out and accepted. Vice President Bush is on the hook, as it were."

Raising his eyes slowly to meet my glare (and I was again visibly angry), he mumbled something about how he had to attend the opening in Madrid of a new United Nations information office and that the king himself was going to be there.

"And how much money does the king of Spain give you?" I asked with an extra-heavy dose of sarcasm.

"I don't really know right off."

"Well, Don Javier, the vice president of the United States, representing the U.S. government, can bankrupt the UN by encouraging Senator Kassebaum to really cut the UN budget drastically."

"Oh," he replied sheepishly, "that Jewish woman wouldn't do that, would she?"

I left Don Javier's office in a real funk, waited about half an hour in my office to cool off, and then asked to get Jenny Fitzgerald on the line.

"Jenny, I don't know how to tell you this, but this jerk we have for a secretary-general has just stiffed us. He alleges that on March 15 he has a previous rendezvous with the king of Spain, no less."

"Pedro, just a second," said Jenny. The next voice I heard was Bush's.

"What's this? He's welching after we got all those Senate folks invited? The king of Spain? I don't understand!"

"Neither do I, sir, except that Javier has gotten it inside his thimble-sized brain cavity, where his pea brain bounces around, that Nancy Kassebaum is a Jew, and it appears he doesn't like Jews."

"I don't believe a word you say, Pedro," the vice president said.

"Well, it's true, and little does he know that the king of Spain, in spite of being a Bourbon, is indirectly related to King Ferdinand of Aragon, who was illegitimate and whose mother was Jewish."

"Okay, Pedro, I understand. It's fairy-tale territory up there. Don't give it a thought. You did the right thing from the start. We won't have any problem alleging some sort of conflict. Don't worry!"

Later the Peruvian patriarch had the temerity to suggest that a meeting with the president of the United States would be perhaps more appropriate for a UN secretary-general.

"The president is Jewish," I said sarcastically, "and so is his secretary of defense!"

Nothing daunted, Don Javier used his other "official" channels to arrange a visit to Washington and a meeting with Reagan in the White House at 12:45 P.M. several months later. A week prior to that "momentous event," Don Javier told me and everyone within sight in the UN Secretariat that Ronald Reagan had asked him over for lunch.

In fact, Reagan arrived at the meeting, which was held outside the Oval Office, after a twenty-minute delay. He spent five minutes with Don Javier and then excused himself, telling the Peruvian anti-Semite that he, Reagan, had a luncheon appointment to keep.

CHAPTER SIX

The U.S. Intelligence Counterparts

I n 1984, when I first came to the UN, Ambassador Kirkpatrick had agreed that I needed an instant and reliable conduit so I could pass on to our own intelligence people whatever information I was able to glean about Soviet intelligence collection activities and similar violations of the "sanctity" of the UN Secretariat. Jeane had already put me in touch with the CIA officer at the U.S. mission, Janine Bruckner.

For the CIA officials in Washington, with whom I began to meet about once a month, it was just a routine job and a chance to get away from the depressing Langley, Virginia, environment. We would meet in Georgetown at an undistinguished venue called the American Café. There, they kept asking me the same exasperating questions over and over again.

These perfunctory sessions were a total waste of time and not worth the effort I had to make to travel to Washington. Soon it was decided that a special CIA representative would meet me in New York for my convenience at another undistinguished emporium to ask me the same repetitive and inane questions.

Jeane's conduits at the State Department had already proved to be useless, for the department had two stock replies to any revelations I might transmit through her: "We already know that," which was a lie, or "We don't want to raise these types of issues [i.e., espionage] because that would threaten bilateral relations with the Soviet Union." The third excuse for their indifference—that such additional concerns might make someone miss taking his wife to the supermarket after regular State Department working hours—was never tendered, for obvious reasons. What we needed, Jeane seemed to feel, was a more practical contact, a direct channel to the FBI.

Jeane Kirkpatrick's clout in the Department of State was practically nonexistent. She was an academic who had written an article, "Dictatorships and Double Standards," that Ronald Reagan greatly admired. As a result, Reagan asked her to be our woman at the UN. Finding most of the programs of UN agencies like UNESCO (culture) and WIPO (intellectual property) to be outrageously politicized, Jeane spoke out openly as often as she could, denouncing the perversion of the UN's nonideological mission. The State Department found this behavior appalling and her imposition of an American spy in the UN Secretariat (yours truly) an additional offense against the decorum required in the practice of diplomacy.

In all fairness, the Cold War was thawing from the middle 1980s on, and the menace of an irresistible Soviet Union was becoming less and less of an obsession in the media and even in certain government circles in Washington. Those were the days of decrepit Soviet leadership that preceded the reformist leadership of Mikhail Gorbachev.

Jeane Kirkpatrick's deputy in those days was Charles Lichenstein. He was very aggressive and occasionally clamorous in his contempt for the UN as a legitimate international forum. Lichenstein arranged a meeting between myself and James Fox, head of the FBI's New York office. We had our first meeting in Washington at the Justice Department.

Fox was a delight. He understood perfectly the problem that I, and by extension, Jeane, faced in channeling the information I was able to unearth on a continuing basis. In other words, placing an American spy in the UN Secretariat had been long overdue. On the other hand, not having an effective government channel that could circumvent the apathy of the State Department remained unwise and wasteful.

I mentioned this to Vice President Bush in a session in his Senate office, and he agreed that the processes of monitoring the activities of my Soviet counterparts and passing on significant developments should occur via the director of the FBI's New York office. That made me a legitimate and legal counterspy, one who spied on the spies who were spying on my country.

Fox made arrangements for me to meet weekly with an FBI agent in New York. We agreed that he and any of his colleagues would identify themselves as "Mr. Mason" on the phone, a fictitious name I would easily recognize. From mid-1984 on, I had lunch at FBI expense once a week at a nondescript pub at Fifty-third Street and Second Avenue.

Fox cautioned me not to expect too much from these frequent exchanges. He knew all too well that the big stuff, the big picture of Soviet violations of the "neutrality" of the UN Secretariat and any other type of corruption at the UN, required in-place investigation—that is, catching people in the act, acquiring UN documents, even arresting people. All of which the FBI was not allowed to do, for the UN Secretariat enjoyed diplomatic immunity. Besides, UN premises were already being used by a regiment of undercover KGB operatives. The UN Secretariat, Jim explained with a devious smile, would become too crowded if the FBI also got into the act.

"Pedro," Fox said, "we have tried numerous times in the past to catch common criminals with the goods right there in the UN premises. Most famous of these futile episodes was an attempt we made a few years ago to intercept heavy drug trafficking in the UN Secretariat garage. We know that diplomatic limousines and New York drug dealers, designated as guests of different missions, still park side by side in the UN basement and, in a leisurely fashion, exchange quantities of narcotics for briefcases full of money in plain view. We tried to catch them, and to do that we had to get permission from the State Department. The department, in turn, sought permission from your secretary-general. By the time the word got around and we were allowed to perform a quick inspection of the holy UN premises, there wasn't a drug dealer in sight. So, you see the problem."

My personal secretary for a time was an Italian-American woman from Queens who had friends among the UN guards and eventually married one of them. Among her acquaintances was another Italian-American, a guard who would come to our office periodically and hang around. He flattered me on occasion by saying that I was the only American in the Secretariat that he enjoyed talking to.

One time he asked, after hesitating, if I would someday consider having lunch with him. I replied, "Who's paying?" "Oh, my treat, sir!" he said. "What about right now?" I suggested, and we were off.

During lunch I mentioned what I had heard about the drug scene in the UN garage. "Oh, sure," he said, "it goes on all the time. The embassy limos from those countries where there is access to cocaine, heroin, and other quality products—not pot, that's low-end stuff—come in and park in the area reserved for diplomats. They choose a space with a vacant parking place next to it. Then some car with a fake guest parking permit comes in and parks beside the limo. Both trunks fly open. From one is withdrawn a sack of money and from the other the high-quality stuff. The exchange is made, and the guest car drives away with the goods."

"And where do the bad guys take the stuff?" I inquired.

"Well, I guess to the New York public schools where dealers are waiting, or to downtown distributors. Wherever they can sell it. Do you want to see those guys in action? I'll take you by on the way back from lunch. Just do me a favor and don't stare at the transactions, if we see any. It's better to ignore what those people do, if you know what I mean! I may be a UN guard, but I value my life."

We did what he proposed and, as promised, two black limos, in different places in the diplomatic parking area in the UN garage, both with their trunks open, were flanked by two sedans, also with open trunks. Although I did not stare, the operations were exactly as Jim Fox had described.

"I never thought we would see those guys performing on cue!" I said to my new friend as we moved further away from the scene. "Oh, yeah," he said, "it's a regular UN institution and a damn good business, you know."

My contacts with successive FBI special agents—all named Mason—lasted for the next fourteen years, both while I was still at the UN and later out of it as head of an institute related to the UN. The meetings always followed the same pattern. The big intelligence items—such as the fact that the Finnish undersecretary-general for administration, Martti Ahtisaari, was probably cooperating with the Soviets—were noted by my FBI friends with due solemnity. But what they really wanted to know were the minutiae. Did a certain Ignatiev bring two overcoats to the office, leaving one on a coat hanger while he snuck out at midday wearing the other? Did crafty Perevertsev take long vacations during which his whereabouts were unaccounted for?

Judging from the evidence, none of these suspected "spies" was ever officially identified as such, and the U.S. government never, while I was at the UN, declared any of them persona non grata and asked that they leave. One would surmise that the FBI was not too successful at catching any of them with the goods. They were fully "accredited" spies, as it were, although their "espionage" activities—if we deign to call them that—were of the intelligence-gathering variety, with very little in the way of actual secret-stealing.

Yet in intelligence circles—our own, the British, the old German Bundesnachrichtendienst, or the even more relaxed French Deuxième Bureau—it has been well known that gathering large quantities of material from any and all sources nets much more valuable information than the dangerous and dubious pastime of hard-core espionage. Stolen "secrets" are usually of doubtful origin, involve very questionable sources, and often yield reliable information from a very unreliable and compromised source . . . or vice versa. I had learned that early in my career investigating Soviet and Eastern European defectors during the late 1950s, when I interacted with our friendly foreign intelligence counterparts in Germany.

So the Soviets' largest-by-far intelligence operation in the United States, and the most successful—as it has been described to me by very complicit Russians after the fall of the USSR—was their collection effort based in the UN Secretariat. This was totally contrary to the status agreement between the United States as host country and the United Nations. It violated the most basic theorems of the UN Charter. It was thoroughly contrary to the national security interests of the United States. And it was an outrageous, illegal activity in which, as we have seen, the U.S. State Department had no special interest, particularly not if that additional concern could interfere with shopping hours at the neighborhood Safeway or Giant supermarkets.

The busy-bee "spy" operations I conducted in the UN, and similar services I provided my FBI friends for several years after leaving the UN Secretariat, earned me, as I have said, a lovely plaque from the next director of the New York FBI office after the untimely death of James Fox. I was described in the colorful metal plaque as patriotic, etc., instead of somebody who carried out the functions of a pest, an embarrassment to the more world-wise, laissez-faire elements in the American foreign policy establishment.

During the administration of President George H. W. Bush, my communications with the State Department did improve, though not right away. Diplomatic success at the UN involves the ability to get along, for the UN is, after all, an international organization. Everyone in the State Department agreed that Jeane Kirkpatrick was too much of an "intellectual" to understand the benign essence of diplomacy.

Unfortunately, Kirkpatrick's successor as U.S. permanent representative, General Vernon (Dick) Walters, had one main goal, and he continued to state it for anyone who would listen. It was to "repair" the "damage" that Jeane had done. Walters claimed to be making friends for the U.S. wherever Jeane had "alienated" delicate and sensitive people. But the Bush administration also appointed a former Justice Department official to the position of assistant secretary for international organizations at the State Department who fully understood Walters's windbag proclivities. His name was John Bolton, and we first met in Washington at the office of my fellow Basque, Senator Paul Laxalt.

John immediately realized that gathering inside information at the upper levels of the Secretariat was a matter of considerable significance if the U.S. was to hold its own at the UN. He did not see the Secretariat as a particularly funny joke, in spite of the indifference of the rest of the State Department to the use being made of the larger UN organization with branches all over the world as a propaganda weapon against the United States, and as an intelligence collection headquarters for the Soviets inside the United States. John did understand the absurdity of maintaining and supporting a place like the UN as a law unto itself, rife with nepotism, incompetence, corruption, and thriving in a sea of anti-Semitism and love-hate for the host country and the host city. He presented this picture at all congressional hearings on the UN.

Walters soon capitulated and deferred to Bolton's more focused approach to U.S. relations with the Third World through what was, to a large degree, a pretentious aggregation of thinly disguised scoundrels.

I saw John regularly in his State Department digs and talked to him on the phone even more frequently. His interest in the circuslike goings-on at the UN never flagged. On one occasion he told me that the news I had conveyed to him was totally corroborated by information he had received the day before from the FBI. I pointed out that it was not surprising, for I was the one who had informed the FBI two days before that.

Bolton was principally responsible with the support of Secretary of State Lawrence Eagleburger for the repeal by the UN General Assembly of the obnoxious Zionism-equals-Racism resolution.

CHAPTER SEVEN

The Anti-Semitic UN Culture

Early on in my UN experience, Emilio de Olivares, the secretary-general's Peruvian executive assistant, had confronted me with an aggravating question:

"¿Pedro, tu eres judío o solo judaizante?" ["Pedro, are you a Jew or just a Jew-lover?"]

Back then I had wondered whether there was some secret quota that specified the exact percentage of Americans of Jewish background allowed in the UN Secretariat. This could have explained the early obsession with my Jewishness. If I were Jewish, I would seem to be above the quota. I also wondered whether some informal understanding to this effect did not exist between the U.S. State Department and the UN. The department clearly recognized the need not to raise the issue in view of its "sensitivity," just as in the early 1960s it had no Jews in its own European Bureau so as not to offend its European clients—a matter that Robert Kennedy and I brought up at the time with Secretary of State Dean Rusk and Averell Harriman.

Maybe the author should explain why, as a non-Jew, he feels so strongly about anti-Semitism. Jews have been frequently criticized as not doing enough to denounce and combat anti-Semitism wherever it takes place. After all, the incoherent and cowardly antipathy toward Jews should be a matter for Jews to protest and fight against.

Although I do not deny that Jews, deeply religious or merely bound by a tradition, would be expected to oppose anti-Semitism in any of its varied manifestations, I most certainly do not agree that combating anti-Semitism is the exclusive responsibility of Jews. Anti-Semitism thrives in the absence of Jews. What's more, anti-Semitic feelings are seldom expressed in the presence of Jews. Since Jews are anything but ubiquitous, surrogates have to take up the fight.

But beyond that tactical consideration, there is the moral compulsion that non-Jews have to oppose an odious and dangerous prejudice held and disseminated by non-Jews. Knowing as I do the devastating effects of unchallenged anti-Semitism, I feel strongly that it is my responsibility to fight anti-Semitism wherever and in every way I can—for the very obvious reason that I am not a Jew.

I see the Arab-Israeli problem that continues to fester more than half a century after the end of World War II as a tragic by-product of European disrespect not only for Jews but for the badly mismanaged and exploited, subjugated people of the Middle East, transferred from Ottoman rule to British, French, and Greek colonial control. Israel is the final product of the hypocrisy of European countries—not just Germany and Austria—that bewailed the Holocaust but did not make a move to restore displaced Jews to their homeland and return their confiscated properties after the war ended. Although my pro-Israel sympathies were taken for granted at the UN, my Jewishness was eventually discounted. This made a considerable difference. *Judaizantes* were tolerated as incongruous insiders. Jews, on the other hand, were virtually outside the UN pale—so a few token Jews among the American contingent of four-hundred-plus professionals were regarded as more than enough.

As I have noted, the UN atmosphere is heavy with anti-Semitism, especially in the Secretariat. It is palpable everywhere because there have been so few Jews, Israelis or otherwise, on the Secretariat staff. The anti-Semitic joke, therefore, has been popular, frequent, and always safe there.

"Byl Yevrei . . ." begins the Russian staff member in typical Russian anecdotal style. "There was once a Jew . . ."

"Había un judío . . ." says the Argentine.

Anti-Semitism always flourishes in the absence of Jews. That absence is deafening in the halls and offices of the UN Secretariat. Yes, indeed, a few Jews who try to be accepted as professional members of the UN staff—the tokens—may say that this oppressive, anti-Semitic influence is not ubiquitous, not that bad. However, they are marked men and women—marked as Jews—and discretion is easy to exercise in their presence.

Such discretion is more difficult before the clerical UN staff, which, recruited in the United States, consists of a higher percentage of Jews than the small number who have been able to penetrate the UN professional ranks. Ask one of my former secretaries, who still fears losing her UN retirement and would prefer to remain anonymous. Ask Sonia Nosenbaum, driven almost to distraction by being just "too" Jewish to blend successfully into the mainstream of the UN Secretariat.

The atmosphere of blatant anti-Semitism is palpable not only in everyday verbal exchanges and informal social gatherings in corridors, cafeterias, and dining rooms, but it is also a cosmetic or visual element.

For example, the only work of art worthy of attention in the UN Secretariat building was a magnificent stained-glass mural executed by Marc Chagall that used to grace the staff entrance to the UN building, the most heavily traversed passage in the headquarters complex at the UN. Now the Chagall stained-glass mural languishes in obscurity in a little noticed "chapel" out of sight near the visitors' entrance where insufficient light fails to bring out Chagall's fanciful figures in their characteristic, dominant blues and reds.

It cost a great deal of money to make the change, but former secretary-general Kurt Waldheim, the unrepentant war criminal, did not want a work by a Jewish painter so prominently displayed. That was not what the UN was about—a Jewish theme—he noted. Indeed not. But the Chagall stained-glass work was not a Jewish theme any more than Beethoven's Fifth is a German symphony.

Did the prevailing anti-Semitic culture at the UN Secretariat influence UN policies against Israel? Absolutely! The anti-Semitic culture in the UN Secretariat did not merely reflect the anti-Semitic, anti-Israeli temper of the UN General Assembly. It reflected as well the fact that anti-Semitism has been a continuous state of mind throughout the United Nations, the Secretariat, the General Assembly, and everywhere else, particularly vividly manifested in UN agencies like UNESCO, UNIDO, WIPO, and others.

It is well known, for example, that UNESCO was taken over during the 1960s and '70s by violently anti-Israel political elements that, with the encouragement of UNESCO's director, made the agency a platform for constant criticism of Israel. With a sham veneer of archaeological, anthropological, pseudo-cultural, and scholarly subterfuge and mumbo-jumbo, UNESCO concentrated its campaign on "establishing" that Israel had no place in Palestine and no role in the Middle East other than as a usurping, alien power operating on behalf of corrupt foreign interests in the United States. This from an agency headquartered in Paris that received more than a third of its budget from the United States. The supposedly apolitical agency's behavior was so thoroughly anti-Semitic as to shock even urbane Europeans accustomed to a long tradition of tolerance for anti-Semitism.

At last, the impervious disinterest of the U.S. Congress to the political goings-on at the UN was pierced by the growing UNESCO scandal; the U.S. resigned from UNESCO and withdrew its share of funding.

The UNESCO episode was treated by the American and European press as an outrageous deviation from the accepted norm of UN political neutrality. Accordingly, once the U.S. left UNESCO, everybody on the Hill breathed a sigh of relief. Anti-Semitism at the UN had been dealt with. Of course, the UNESCO phenomenon was not an isolated instance but a virulent manifestation of a systemic disease that has affected all other UN agencies, especially UNIDO (the United Nations Industrial Development Organization), WIPO (the World Intellectual Property Organization), and Human Rights.

There has long been strong support in the U.S. Congress for Israel. Public opinion in the United States and in both political parties has consistently condemned anti-Semitism here and abroad. Yet the role of the U.S. Department of State with respect to the anti-Semitic culture of the UN has been one of diplomatic indifference.

Individual U.S. permanent representatives like Arthur Goldberg, Daniel Patrick Moynihan, Jeane Kirkpatrick, and Lawrence Eagleburger have sounded forth with righteous thunder against General Assembly resolutions and UNESCO policies condemning Israel, especially the infamous G.A. Resolution 3379, passed in 1975 (and only recently repealed), denouncing Zionism as a form of racism. Israel has been rejected by every regional grouping, including the European regional association of common interests, as if everyone in the world concurred that Israel was a diseased society that nobody should touch. This anti-Semitism was rampant at the UN while repeated official apologies and protestations year in and year out deploring the Holocaust were made outside the UN by European nations like Germany, France, Sweden, Poland, Italy, Hungary, Austria, Romania, and others.

But the atmosphere of outspoken anti-Semitism, well established in the very marrow of the entire UN organization, has been left completely undisturbed by the U.S. State Department. That atmosphere goes along with the suspicion that the United States is ruled by Jews—its government, the media, the business sector, the academic community, and everywhere else. Javier Pérez de Cuellar had awkwardly suggested at one point that I could be of great value as a liaison with Jewish "elements" in Washington. But since I did not reply to his suggestion, he never specified in what capacity I could conduct such a liaison, which was really just as well.

Nevertheless, I took advantage of my general mandate from Don Javier to talk to Congressman James Scheuer and his staff, and to Senator D'Amato's staff, emphasizing the need to make the State Department confront the Secretariat on its glaring anti-Semitic practices and to insist on filling the Israeli quota on the Secretariat staff, an outrageous omission that endured year after year.

I first learned about the repeated rejection of Israeli candidates for Secretariat staff positions from Israeli ambassador Benjamin (Bibi) Netanyahu.

Netanyahu, being both U.S.-educated and not a career diplomat, was less tolerant of the ostracism of Israel at the UN than many of his Israeli predecessors. He had no problem speaking out against the conditions that I describe. He did so in public forums in New York and in other parts of the country, and thus was able to make powerful friends in the United States, political friends who supported Israel. Netanyahu had the total confidence and cooperation of Jeane Kirkpatrick and was the principal reason Mayor Koch in New York repeatedly referred to the UN as a "cesspool." But the U.S. and the UN were two separate forums. Outside the UN, Netanyahu acted as the ambassador extraordinary of Israel, much more effective and sought after than the official Israeli ambassador to the White House. Netanyahu was not a diplomat, he was a man of substance—a statesman.

On the other hand, at the UN, Netanyahu had no influence at all. As a matter of fact, as a vocal Israeli, Netanyahu was ostracized even more as a "dangerous troublemaker." The more articulate he was, the more unacceptable. It was with typical cowardly circumspection that the secretary-general made only oblique references to my Israeli connection via Netanyahu.

"Watch out for that Netanyahu," the indiscreet Olivares said more boldly to me once in the presence of the discreet secretary-general.

"You watch out for Netanyahu yourself, and for me along with him. Your official duties, whatever they are, do not include interfering in my personal business!" I replied. Don Javier confined himself to a pained expression betraying his dislike of controversy.

It had been only a few months after my arrival in the never-never land of the UN Secretariat when Jeane Kirkpatrick introduced me at a U.S. mission social function to Netanyahu, recently arrived as the UN permanent representative from Israel.

"This is the only American we can trust in the UN Secretariat,"

Jeane said to Netanyahu. Then she turned to me and winked. "Look after the ambassador's interests over there, will you, Pedro?"

I nodded, saying, "There appear to be no high-level Jews in the whole Secretariat."

Bibi smiled, put his hand on my shoulder, and quipped, "You are the only high-level Jew there."

"I hate to disappoint you, but I'm really not a Jew," I explained.

"That is precisely my point," said Bibi.

After looking around for any goings-on in the Secretariat that I thought might affect Israel's interests, I finally decided to establish direct contact. The UN Charter theoretically frowns on UN member state missions influencing officials of the UN Secretariat, but it has nothing against Secretariat officials informing or even influencing member state missions. Needless to say, the spectacle of 274 Soviet and an equal or greater number of Soviet satellite member state Secretariat staff members getting their daily marching orders at their respective missions had long ago rendered the UN Charter's authority moot in every sense.

The UN Israeli mission on the fifteenth floor of a nondescript office building near Forty-second Street on Second Avenue was, and still is, a vivid illustration of Israel's plight at the UN, which has long been, in effect, regarded as enemy territory. When you visited the mission you had to travel first to the fourteenth floor, then change elevators to one that went only to the fifteenth floor. I was definitely expected as I arrived on 15 and faced a cylindrical compartment that I was instructed to enter by a remote, hidden speaker. The cylinder closed, and I became aware that something or someone was checking me out, for I was kept in this confining space for a couple of minutes, a long time to spend in a cylinder. Presumably after I had been checked for identity confirmation and any hidden devices or weapons on my person, the cylindrical sliding door in the back of the compartment opened. As I stepped out, I was met by two guards. They escorted me past people sitting at desks who gave me suspicious glances as I passed.

Finally I arrived at the door of an office that appeared to be the ultimate destination. Behind it, in a room with heavy bars on the windows, sat Benjamin Netanyahu.

"Why do you have such heavy bars on your windows, Bibi? This is, after all, the fifteenth floor, way above street level, and this is New York, not the Gaza Strip."

"Because, my fine feathered friend, some of my less tolerant colleagues at the UN might well get the idea of dropping in from the sixteenth floor," Bibi said. "It has been tried. Or of lobbing at the end of a rope an explosive device, also from the sixteenth floor. So we put these crossed bars on the windows to prevent that!"

Thanks to Netanyahu's effective outside lobbying, several U.S. congressmen and senators knew from his firsthand accounts about the outrageous pariah status of Israel at the UN.

Senator D'Amato, an Italian-American senator with a large Jewish constituency, was particularly attentive to the problem, and in 1986, after the scandal broke about Kurt Waldheim's Nazi past, he called me personally to see if I could have the UN open up the Waldheim files that the Secretariat maintained as classified documents.

The Waldheim files, held in a sealed state by the UN, consisted of background material on former secretary-general Kurt Waldheim that revealed interesting details concerning his youthful Nazi proclivities in Austria and his wartime criminal role in Yugoslavia. Material in these files was surely not different from more extensive files held by the U.S. government and, without doubt, also by the Soviet government, which both sides refused to make public and denied having.

Waldheim's membership in the Hitlerjugend organization and his implementation, as a staff officer in Yugoslavia, of orders from top Wehrmacht authorities for the execution of British prisoners of war, were details well known to both the Americans and the Soviets in 1971, when their affirmative votes clinched Waldheim's appointment. That appointment was made by the UN Security Council and ratified by the UN General Assembly—the latter always a mere formality.

How could a Nazi war criminal have been chosen as UN secretary-general by the U.S. and the Soviets? Let us rephrase the question. How could the U.S. and the Soviets have passed up a chance to have as a UN secretary-general someone who was as subject to intimidation and blackmail as Kurt Waldheim, a man with a hidden Nazi and war criminal past? Put this way, the question seems appropriately rhetorical.

In 1987, after Waldheim was refused a third term as UN secretary-general and ran successfully for president of Austria, the United States put him on a "watchlist" of unacceptable foreigners not allowed reentry into the United States. That would have been a precarious step for the United States to take, to declare the head of state of a friendly nation effectively persona non grata, had there not been sufficient supporting evidence in U.S. files corroborating what was in the UN files.

Why were the files sealed in the first place? This was part of the policy of secrecy with which all UN documents are treated by the UN. Besides which, the eleven-nation agreement that consigned the Waldheim files to the UN repository stipulated that the files would not be released to the public without unanimous consent of all the parties. Did D'Amato want the files opened so he could shore up his hypothetical Jewish vote in New York while running in a campaign against a Jewish opponent? Perhaps, but in discussions I had much later with D'Amato, his candor and typical vehemence in condemning the anti-Israeli policies of the UN indicated to me that he resented the anti-Semitic and anti-American tendencies at the UN on a very genuine and personal basis.

I therefore went to see Don Javier on D'Amato's behalf and put the senator's request to him bluntly: "Either you open the files to the public and let D'Amato have his way, or during this year's New York Senate election campaign, D'Amato will clobber the UN and further reduce the U.S. contribution already lowered by the U.S. Congress."

"But I can't release those files until the eleven nations that signed the original agreement to keep them locked up agree to release them," Don Javier said, trying to look helpless.

"Yes, you can! You are the UN secretary-general. So you just unseal the Waldheim garbage can, and none of the eleven signatories will dare open their mouths or even recall that they signed anything. Do it!"

Giving the pusillanimous Don Javier a little credit—though not too much—he did release the files. I notified D'Amato's administrative assistant and answered a query from the *Forward*, New York's Jewish newspaper. I said that D'Amato's pressure had brought about the release.

Word quickly spread throughout the Secretariat that I was a friend of D'Amato's—a "serious" accusation at the supposedly apolitical UN. Javier—fearful of being thought disloyal to his infamous Nazi predecessor—told me in the hall outside his office that everyone claimed that I was D'Amato's close friend, thus trying to lay entirely on me his mildly courageous action on the Waldheim files. "I am!" I said, exaggerating my relationship with D'Amato.

Mark Green, New York City ombudsman and later a candidate for mayor, was then running for the Senate against D'Amato. He subsequently called to ask if the UN was taking sides in the New York senatorial campaign.

"No," I said. "I stated to the press the fact that the Waldheim files were opened as a consequence of D'Amato's request. Had anyone else called first, I would have given that person all the credit."

Javier had no understanding of the subtleties of American politics nor the foggiest idea who Mark Green was. The Peruvian expatriate was able to identify D'Amato only vaguely, without any awareness that the senator was chairman of the Senate Banking Committee and without any idea of what the committee did or could mean to the UN.

Periodically, with Javier's blithe wave-of-the-hand approval, I would meet in Washington with Sen. Nancy Kassebaum's staff and recommend that the senator put more emphasis on the anti-Semitic, anti-Israeli practices at the UN Secretariat and also on the blatantly high degree of corruption there.

Senator Kassebaum had a distinguished record as a fiscal watchdog and maintained a staff that had extensive credentials in looking at wasted government funds. The issue of fighting government waste resonated quite well with the senator's constituents in Kansas. With the arrival on her staff a few years before of a legislative assistant named Christensen, who became interested in the lack of accountability of the UN on all budgetary issues, the senator latched onto the UN, not on policy grounds, but as an example of the U.S. government's waste of U.S. taxpayers' money.

The Kansas senator's cuts in the U.S. contribution (from 25 percent of the overall UN Secretariat budget to 20 percent) were justified on grounds of simple waste and inefficiency—the UN's inability to administer its financial resources. Kassebaum's preoccupation with the UN was not in response to any promptings from me. But I urged that the unjustifiable and blatantly illegal practice of keeping Israelis out of the Secretariat and the patent thievery throughout the Secretariat should also be highlighted by Kassebaum to help make all this a more public issue.

At one point, Don Javier and I were discussing the hostility in the U.S. Senate toward the United Nations. I was trying to explain why different senators had problems with the UN. That is when he said, "Senator Kastenbaum [sic] of course hates us because she is Jewish."

"Senator Nancy Kassebaum from Kansas is an Episcopalian," I explained. "She is the daughter of Alf Landon, a former presidential candidate. She is not Jewish. It seems, Don Javier, that anybody you don't like in the UN is accused of being Jewish."

"Well," said Javier, looking out of one of his six windows, as was his wont when confronted with anything that made him uncomfortable, "if she is not Jewish, the people who vote for her are. Who was this Lyndon? Not like the president?"

It was no use to try to explain that Kansas is not one of the major U.S. Jewish centers.

"No, Don Javier. Alf Landon ran for president against Franklin Roosevelt and lost. He has no relationship to Lyndon Johnson."

Later on Pérez de Cuellar, following his anti-Semitic inclinations, refused still another request for an appointment from the president of the Anti-Defamation League made through me. "I finally had to see the president of B'nai B'rith this year. All those Jewish organizations are the same. I mustn't see too many of them for political reasons, you know," Javier confided in me.

"All the grade school children that bring you doves of peace," I said, "are also all the same, but you find time in your busy schedule to see them over and over again. Some of them must be Jewish. Perhaps that could cause you some political embarrassment as well."

Javier, as I had already learned, never got angry. He just got flustered, and to relieve his fluster, he had six windows to look out of facing New York's East River estuary and the Pepsi-Cola sign in Long Island City.

But Javier was hardly alone at the UN in seeing Jews under every bed. In 1987, for example, Sen. John Heinz of Pennsylvania proposed an amendment to the foreign affairs legislation that contained the U.S. contribution to the UN to cut off funds to the UN. Almost everyone in the UN Secretariat "knew" that this was because Senator Heinz (later killed in a plane crash) was Jewish. He was not. For more than a hundred years the Heinz family had been major contributors to Protestant causes.

The same year, a former executive of the Canadian Broadcasting Corporation, Thérèse Sevigny, was made undersecretary-general for public information, the UN department with the largest budget and a correspondingly large staff. A year later, she was asked in Washington by Congressman Scheuer of New York if she had any Israelis on her staff. She said she didn't know, but she had a Jew, which she pronounced "chew." Did she think American Jews and Israelis were all the same? Scheuer asked her. "To me, all Chews are the same," she replied.

The congressman raised objections to her statement, so she gave a press conference in her UN office in New York and essentially repeated the same thing all over again, adding something to the effect that of course she was not anti-Semitic, but after all, Jews were Jews.

Her statements had understandably made Scheuer quite angry, and I was sent by Javier to talk to the congressman.

I told Scheuer's staff that the lady meant what she said, that the UN Secretariat thought nothing of it, and that as far as I could tell, neither did the U.S. State Department.

"Here is an opportunity to raise a big fuss," I advised. "Demand to get the names of the Israeli members on the UN Secretariat staff. You won't find one."

Scheuer made the appropriate fuss, and word got back to the

secretary-general that it was all my doing. But the timid Peruvian said nothing, and that was all that really mattered.

In the midst of the excitement in the UN Secretariat about my Scheuer, D'Amato, and Kassebaum connections, a new undersecretary-general for administration was appointed, a Finn of very ample proportions whose name was Martti Ahtisaari. Not long after Mr. Ahtisaari's arrival, I noticed that he paid daily visits to one Vassily Safronchuk, the new Soviet undersecretary-general for political and Security Council affairs. Most members of the UN Secretariat staff, even some of the Soviets themselves, joked that Ahtisaari had been properly "Finlandized," referring to domination by the powerful Soviet Union over its puny northern neighbor.

Mr. Ahtisaari in turn had his own vassal, a certain Tapio Kanninen, a Finnish UN staff member working in the office of the secretary-general. Ahtisaari's Finnish compatriot attempted, and quite frequently succeeded, in getting fairly sensitive information from the U.S. government on behalf of the secretary-general. In fact, the information went directly to Ahtisaari.

One day Kanninen had the scatterbrained idea of sending a letter on behalf of the secretary-general to the Stanford Research Institute, a U.S. Department of Defense contractor, asking again for the firing sequence of U.S. intercontinental missiles in case of a nuclear exchange with the USSR. Kanninen had heard that SRI did frequent war-gaming exercises for Defense.

SRI sent the letter to Undersecretary of Defense Fred Iklé, my former U.S. Arms Control Agency boss and a good friend. Iklé called me. I told him to send a copy of the letter to Senator William Roth, chairman of the Senate Intelligence Committee. Roth demanded an explanation, and Javier, still UN secretary-general, sent me to explain matters to Roth.

And so I did. I told Roth that it was all part of Ahtisaari's internal intelligence operation on behalf of his Soviet masters, and that it was as absurd as it was funny. Of course, it was totally out of line with the legitimate activities the UN Secretariat was expected to perform, which did not include doing espionage work for the USSR.

"Should we cut the UN budget some more?" Roth asked. "By all means," I said, "but make a political point when you do so. Don't say it's just because the UN wastes money."

Word got back to the secretary-general that Roth was furious about the Kanninen letter, as were several other senators, including Robert Kasten, Nancy Kassebaum, and Fritz Hollings.

In a less-than-brilliant move, Javier asked none other than the broad-beamed Ahtisaari to visit the aggrieved senators. To all of them Ahtisaari explained that cutting the U.S. contribution to the UN was out of the question.

"Finland, where I come from, pays it debts," Ahtisaari lectured Senator Hollings. "The United States, committed by treaty to fund its share of the UN budget, should do as Finland does."

"An' what's the national budget of Finland, Mr. Attsarara?" asked Hollings. Ahtisaari quoted a modest figure.

"Well, when your budget gets to be the size of ours, ya'll come to see me again, ya hear!"

Several of these senators told Ahtisaari that UN Secretary-General Javier Pérez de Cuellar should send me to talk to them because I understood how to deal with the Senate.

The broad-beamed Ahtisaari came back to the UN fuming.

"How is it you know so many senators in Washington and why do you go to see them so often?"

"Let me answer your questions in reverse order. I go to Washington because the secretary-general wants me to. Now, how or why it is that I know so many senators is none of your business any more than it is my business to inquire of you how many Finnish parliamentarians you know.

"But, since you are in charge of administration here at the UN, let me give you a helpful hint," I went on. "You could do much to restore the U.S. contribution to its former 25 percent of the UN budget if you started hiring Israelis to fill the allotted positions the state of Israel is entitled to in the UN Secretariat. That would be a really clever move and would give the UN greater acceptance in Washington as a bona fide international organization and not as an arena for petty political conspiracies."

Ahtisaari, later to become president of Finland, put his hands on his waist, appearing to increase even more his already generous girth, and said, "The only reason Israel is a member of the United Nations is because your country supports it. As far as I am concerned, Israel has even less legitimacy than the PLO, and they only have observer status at the UN!"

Much later on Martti Ahtisaari, now ex-president of Finland, was appointed by UN Secretary-General Kofi Annan as de facto chairman of the UN commission selected to investigate the alleged Jenin massacres. Ahtisaari's anti-Israel reputation had been well established among Israeli politicians during his tour at the UN, before becoming Finland's president. His subsequent appointment to that ill-conceived commission was a deliberate irritant calculated to bring about a predictably negative Israeli reaction. The unmistakably biased character of the Jenin investigation was obvious for anyone in Israel to see.

The smug anti-Semitic culture of the UN Secretariat has never been acknowledged or even recognized by the inmates of that organization. Certainly Javier Pérez de Cuellar, when he refused to give an appointment to the president of B'nai B'rith or when he assumed that Senator Kassebaum was Jewish—because she criticized the United Nations, and all Jews hated the United Nations—did not consider himself anti-Semitic.

Likewise, the Soviet undersecretary-general had felt perfectly at ease within the prevailing culture of the UN Secretariat to try to find out if I was one of those Jews that caused trouble everywhere.

No, the undersecretary-general was not anti-Semitic! What was this anti-Semitic, anyway? They had some Jews in the USSR. They were scientists and doctors, and many of them were connected to the black market. You know how those Jews are!

"You have an obsession in America with the Jewish question. You are so sensitive," a perfectly sincere Soviet anti-Semite said to me at an official UN luncheon held in April 1986 to commemorate the end of the International Year of Peace. "You see everything we Russians say as an example of anti-Semitism. We are not anti-Semitic in my country. We have Jews. Here in America you are run by the Jews. Your government is controlled by the Jews."

Buttressing this "normal" attitude within the UN Secretariat was the UN General Assembly, where an overwhelming majority had passed the infamous resolution denouncing Zionism as racism. There, Yasser Arafat had spoken with a revolver strapped to his waist to the repeated applause of several hundred delegates and observers.

To anyone who may have doubted that a culture of anti-Semitism prevails not only in the UN Secretariat but throughout other UN organizations and some UN-accredited nongovernmental organizations as well, may I point to the disastrous Durban conference (held in 2001) on racism and other forms of abuse and intolerance. There, the issue of Zionism as racism again reared its ugly head, and considerable animus was directed primarily at the United States, Israel's protector.

Critics of the second Bush administration say that it was a mistake to not participate in the Durban debate about Zionism. Whatever foreign policy problems the Bush administration may have had, not taking part in the Durban ambush was not one of them. Nevertheless, on the issue of anti-Semitism, with its direct and powerful UN antecedents, the U.S. has had no influence at the UN because the belief has always prevailed in the UN that Israel is nothing more than an agent of the United States.

On October 15, 1996, I was jaywalking across Forty-second Street in New York, between Second and Third Avenues. Intent on surviving several wayward yellow cabs that seemed determined to hunt me down, I failed to notice that a large crowd was casually marching down Forty-second Street in the same direction.

"What's going on?" I inquired of one of the marchers soon after I reached safe haven across the street.

"It's the Day of Atonement rally in front of the UN building. Come on and see for yourself!"

How could I refuse such a generous invitation? Besides, I was headed to the UN myself for a luncheon at the respectable UN hour of 1:30 P.M. with some members of my former UN staff at the UN cafeteria. The cafeteria is the more "colloquial" gathering place for many pretensionless UN staffers whose sybaritic habits can only be indulged on a budget. The UN cafeteria is heavily subsidized.

As I passed Ralph Bunche Park, I recognized the Reverend Louis Farrakhan, speaking to the large crowd across from the main entrance of the UN on First Avenue. His words conveyed high praise for UN Secretary-General Boutros Boutros-Ghali and condemnation for the policies of Israel in the Middle East.

I passed the UN gate and looked back. Farrakhan and a small group of his companions were now crossing over as well. They passed the gate behind me and were met at the main entrance of the UN building by a fairly large group of people, among whom I recognized several Libyan UN delegates. It was they who greeted Farrakhan.

Once inside, Farrakhan marched across the UN halls like some sort of conquering hero and was hailed and recognized by almost every person he passed. This was a big and not unexpected event, obviously planned in advance. The UN Correspondents Association held a press conference for Farrakhan during which he repeated the same themes he had touched upon in his rally across First Avenue.

I was late for lunch with my old cronies, but from them I learned what practically everyone in the building seemed to know already. Farrakhan was there as a guest of the Libyans and a number of Arab delegations, but also at the direct invitation of Boutros-Ghali. Boutros had been persuaded by some questionable American "advisers" that the Nation of Islam was the core of African-American political power. With Farrakhan's backing, Boutros thought he would have no problem winning the support of the Congressional Black Caucus, with which Boutros had met earlier. He was lobbying desperately to be reelected, or more properly, reselected, for another five-year term as UN secretary-general.

The Congressional Black Caucus in Washington had not been too taken with a UN secretary-general lobbying on the Hill. So now

Boutros was playing his "trump card" by winning the support of the powerful hidden eminence who supposedly controlled the African-American vote in the United States.

This farcical episode said so much about the pathetic predicament of the United Nations, so poignantly dependent on the United States and yet so badly informed as to what makes the gears turn and the wheels go round in Washington and with respect to American politics in general. In addition to those reflections, I also felt considerable outrage at the absurd extremes of inappropriate behavior displayed by Boutros-Ghali, who seemed to have not the remotest idea of what a UN secretary-general may or may not do in trying to influence the internal affairs of a member state.

So I wrote an opinion piece for the *Wall Street Journal* describing Boutros-Ghali as what he was—a desperate egomaniac whoring after reappointment. My opinion piece strongly intimated that Boutros-Ghali sympathized with Farrakhan's anti-Semitism.

On October 30, the day the article came out with sketches of the effigies of Boutros and Farrakhan, Boutros went ballistic.

He sent down one of his assistants with a checkbook and orders to buy up all the *Wall Street Journals* left at the newsstand near the elevators of the UN building, notwithstanding the fact that a block away from the UN several other newsstands were selling the same edition and soon ordering more in anticipation of increased demand from across the street. A growing number of UN staffers kept on buying that same issue of the *Journal* for several days. Boutros also gave orders that the *Wall Street Journal* should not be made available at the UN library.

Boutros had already done something similar, although not to this degree, when still earlier *Time* magazine had published an article critical of the Egyptian Copt. Neither the *Wall Street Journal* nor *Time* was exactly devastated by Boutros's unorthodox scorched-earth policy against the disrespectful American press.

Boutros went ballistic not only immediately after my exposure of his inappropriate behavior and muddled thinking, but he stayed in orbit for a while.

Next, he got in touch with the presidents of as many Jewish organizations as his executive secretary could find in the Manhattan telephone directory and summoned them to a conference at the UN. The president of the International Association of Jewish Lawyers and Jurists called me and asked what was going on at the UN. I said I had no idea, but that he should attend the meeting, and, afterward, if he wanted, he could call me and tell me what Boutros had said.

Thus I learned that Boutros, as I had predicted in my op-ed piece in the *Journal,* had told all the invitees that he, Boutros, was not an anti-Semite because he was married to a Jew—a winning argument! Boutros told them he had sent a memorandum to all office directors and undersecretaries-general working for him, requesting that they reject any anti-Semitic ideas that they might harbor.

That same day, I believe it was November 3, 1996, I proceeded to go to the United Nations for a solitary lunch at the UN delegates dining room, where reservations are required. I passed the gates at the UN without incident, even after deliberately dropping my pass in front of the guards and then ostentatiously flashing it before them as a test. My lunch was also uneventful. Much later I learned that Boutros had taken initial steps to have all sorts of things done to me, the least of which would have been exclusion from UN territory, but that cooler heads around him had prevailed after telling the international autocrat that I might be looking forward to some type of challenge.

I was.

More than all the other elements in the UN espionage-counterespionage saga, what bothered me most during my years there was this unrelenting bigotry.

CHAPTER EIGHT

The End of the Cold War at the UN

From being perceived as a dangerous adversary during my first three years in the UN Secretariat, I gradually came to be regarded by the Soviets first as an interesting fixture who was not about to go away, and subsequently as a potential asset who was perhaps worth befriending. The Soviet Union itself was already undergoing profound changes—even if they went largely undetected by our own CIA—and the looming communist disaster contributed to the softening of the KGB attitude toward me. After all, I was a professional comrade in the same line of work.

As the eighties progressed, I became the object of repeated invitations to "international" conferences and "symposiums" in Moscow, Leningrad, and regional capitals in the USSR. These conferences were all associated with the UN. They were paid for with silly money—nonconvertible ruble funds donated to fulfill the requirements of the assessed Soviet contribution to the UN, but spendable only in the Soviet Union.

For quite a while I politely declined such invitations. I suspected that besides their perhaps sincere friendliness and high-sounding intentions, they might have been part of an effort to suck the fellow they regarded as "Reagan's man" at the UN into some unwitting form of complicity with Soviet propaganda objectives.

Nevertheless, as the months passed, the successors to Kashirin, like Perevertsev and the other well-identified UN KGB operatives—along with their durable boss, Undersecretary-General Viacheslav Ustinov, who had managed to remain at the UN without defecting—began inviting me to social events in New York. I could not refuse these invitations without betraying an exaggerated degree of hostility. It also meant that I was expected to reciprocate.

Ustinov, coming to my house for dinner one night with his wife, lost his way—or his chauffeur did. I repeated the directions to my home in New Rochelle on the phone. He remarked that he hoped he would find his way this time in spite of the wordy and obtuse signs that festooned all American roads. Such a condition did not exist in Russia, where there were very few signs—and very few roads.

"Well, Slava," I said, "if you get lost again, stop and ask the FBI car parked behind you how to get to my place."

"Is that really true? Is there an FBI car following us?" Ustinov asked, pretending to be mildly alarmed.

"Stop and find out!" I repeated with mock emphasis.

He knew all too well that there was.

The ice was definitely broken, and the thought of turning some UN Soviets into defectors briefly crossed my mind, but I put the thought aside since my business was not to encourage my new Soviet "buddies" to do any such thing. In any case, the life of most defectors is very sad.

Starting in 1985, I began to receive invitations to travel to Romania as a guest of the Romanian government. I was informed by the secretary-general that such an honor could not be turned down without giving great offense to the hosts. My trip to Romania was pleasant enough, since I had expressed an interest in seeing some of the old, highly decorated monasteries in Moldavia and was taken to most of them during a period of ten days.

The same type of invitation came with the excuse of reviewing Polish efforts to help celebrate the International Year of Peace, 1985. This resulted in several invitations to Warsaw and Krakow. Next came Czechoslovakia under some similar pretext that sounded harmless enough and in representation of the secretary-general. Actually I was a curiosity as Ronald Reagan's principal "spy" at the UN.

Although I traveled to different parts of the world representing the secretary-general, even to socialist countries like Poland and Romania, I still consistently declined invitations to the Soviet Union, so the Soviets complained.

At last the secretary-general approached the new U.S. ambassador, Vernon Walters, about my strange reticence concerning missions to the Union of Soviet Socialist Republics. Walters, who was never too sure of what or who was on first or on second, asked me over to the U.S. mission for lunch and inquired into why I never traveled to the Soviet Union.

I told him. He protested that he himself was accepting invitations to the communist Mecca, so why shouldn't I? I replied that many overt and covert reasons could be added to what I considered to be my personal choice.

"And what if the secretary-general himself, or I perhaps, asked you to attend one of these conferences in Russia?"

"Well, the secretary-general won't do that because he doesn't dare, and second, because, as you see, he is naively asking you to approach me, forgetting that I supposedly work for him and definitely not for you. Your trying to influence me would violate the basic and most sacred principles of the UN Charter. Have you read it, Dick?" My retorts were getting a tad belligerent, so the convivial Walters adopted a more impartial tone. "Suppose the secretary-general did insist that you go to Russia?"

"Well, Dick, then I would resign. But, rest at ease, Don Javier won't do that."

Well, I was partially wrong, for Don Javier did subsequently ask me to go to the Soviet Union. I was asked to represent him by conferring the UN Medal of Freedom to the three hero cities of World War II: Leningrad, Moscow, and Volgograd (previously named Stalingrad).

These were not conferences or staged propaganda events, but a gesture that I really sympathized with. There had never been any question in my mind that the heroic suffering of the Russian people and the magnificent performance of the Red Army had destroyed the bulk of the Wehrmacht in World War II and saved us all from the threat of Nazi aggression. I had no problem with bestowing on the survivors in these hero cities their well-deserved medals. I touched base with Jeane Kirkpatrick in Washington and with the assistant secretary for international organizations at the State Department as well as with my friend Jim Fox at the FBI, and then proceeded to accept.

Walters called me to congratulate me for my decision, which had nothing at all to do with him, and when I remained silent, he added that he had really called to ask a favor. He was, he said, a collector of lacquered Russian Palekh boxes, and wondered, if I found a particularly extravagant one in Russia, whether I would get it for him. It was a strange request, for Walters himself traveled frequently to the USSR. I said, "Of course." I later found a real prize at a huge flea market on the outskirts of Moscow and presented it to Walters as a gift upon my return.

My first trip to the Soviet Union was quite revealing. I spoke before a large number of "civic" organizations, professional trade unions, and writers' guilds, almost always under a picture of Lenin. I spoke in Russian, which made me a little more popular, and I kept being introduced as "President Reagan's special representative," which I consistently corrected with "No, I am the special representative of the secretary-general of the UN." More often than not, this disclaimer produced sporadic laughter and applause among the audience.

I was also closely watched and constantly escorted by my own, personal KGB control officer and an Intourist hostess to all the great sites I had always wanted to see in Leningrad and Moscow—though not in Volgograd, for other than the World War II diorama at the Mamayev Kurgan monument, where the last battle for Stalingrad was fought, there is nothing worth seeing in Volgograd today, the city having been completely leveled during the war.

I suppose that the Soviet gestures made in my direction during the period of 1987–89 were consistent with the effort to convey a spirit of friendship toward the Reagan administration that was evident in many other areas at that time. The effort was carried out in the traditional Soviet style, especially in my case, for I was the only American counterpart to the KGB at the United Nations, which they considered especially significant.

In short, my chaperons had orders to be very nice—but not to let me out of their sight.

Toilet paper was a distinct luxury in those days in the Soviet socialist paradise. At the Rossia Hotel, which boasts of being the largest in the world, as at every other hotel, you had to haggle with the hall monitor on your floor to get a half-used roll placed in your bathroom as a special courtesy. As soon as I arrived at my hotel room, after an intricate process of registration, I checked the bathroom and found, as I suspected, no toilet paper. So I ran out to the hall monitor sitting at her post next to the elevators and asked her to get me a roll of *toilyetnaya bumaga*. She made a face, and I retired to my room. Within five minutes, Geli Neprovsky, my KGB control, appeared at my door with half a roll of toilet paper.

"How did you know I wanted that?" I asked Geli.

"Okay, okay! Never mind how! Sorry it is only half a roll, but I will search for more," Geli replied, waving his arms in a sign of embarrassment and near despair.

Anything I said to the staff of the hotel (nonexistent except for the hall monitors) would be immediately relayed to Geli, and Geli would rush over to accommodate my whim, thus clearly revealing that I was a most highly regarded prisoner.

The Hermitage, the royal palace at Pushkin, Peterhoff palace, the palace at Pavlovsk, the Russian Museum, the Fortress of Peter and Paul, the Admiralty—all of these I visited in Leningrad. Later on I toured practically the entire Kremlin in Moscow, the monastery at Zagorsk, and many other magnificent historical and artistic monuments. I was being taken around like a big, big shot, President Reagan's special representative, all my disclaimers notwithstanding.

In Leningrad, I was spirited away to the Piskariovska, a huge cemetery that contains 1.2 million victims of the German siege of Leningrad, innocent people of all ages who died of starvation or disease. Displays of sentimentality are bad form, I know, but the lump in my throat grew as I stood before each mound marked for a month in 1941, such as, "April 1941, 50,000; May 1941, 70,000," and so on.

When the tour was over, a reporter from *Izvestia* asked why I had come to the Piskariovska. Instead of saying "Because I was brought here by my KGB handler," I said "Because the Fascists at the gates of Leningrad represented chaos and the heroic people here in Leningrad stood for order—and order won! By their sacrifice, the people of Leningrad saved my children and grandchildren [I did not have any of the latter at that time] from the Fascist threat and preserved our freedom. So I came here to thank the victims."

I thought my reply sounded like a well-meaning but standard sort of spiel. That evening and the next day *Pravda, Izvestia, Komsomolskaya Pravda, Vechernyi Leningrad,* and several local papers in Moscow featured what I said, which was also reported several times in *Vryemia,* the national television news program. I asked Geli, my KGB control, why I was getting so much coverage. "Because you are the first American, President Reagan's special emissary, to say any such thing in Russia."

The alleged prior American silence was quite astounding. Trite though they were, my remarks simply reflected the truth. Why not give people their rightful due when they deserve it?

In Volgograd, as the "special representative" of Ronald Reagan (usually pronounced Ronuald Ryehgin in Russia), I was feasted in a really big way. Met at the airport by the mayor, taken to his large home with a motorcycle escort, I again went through the rounds of speeches before drab-looking professionals and officials, all looking bored even during my displays of oratory in Russian. The second day, the mayor took me on his yacht (such was socialism!) down the Volga to the dam where sturgeon congregated in large numbers, unable to proceed further downstream to the Caspian Sea. Some sturgeon reach over eight meters, or twenty-five feet, in length.

Beluga caviar of the most succulent variety was available almost as an incidental decoration throughout the yacht. I overindulged and later that night became sick, yet I am glad I did. I have never met anyone else who consumed a pound of Beluga caviar in one drawn-out sitting. Soon the mayor got chummy, undid his tie, and asked, in apparent confidence and out of earshot of my KGB big brother, "Tell me why *(pochemu)* you speak Russian?"

"To speak to you, of course!" I replied maliciously. Then I added, "No, I got an advanced degree in Russian studies at an American university and for six years lived with a Russian professor's family, so I learned Russian like one should, among Russians."

The mayor got interested. "And have you read Russian authors in Russian?"

"Yes, it is the best way," I said.

"And have you read Lenin? You know, Lenin wrote a lot, and he wrote very well," the mayor continued.

I admitted proudly that I had read Lenin, although much of it in English translation, and agreed that Lenin was a prolific writer even if he wrote very few short stories and novels. Then, more seriously, I added, "Lev Trotsky, his history of the Russian Revolution, that was quite an experience."

"Never mind Trotsky! He was a Jew and didn't understand anything about the real Russia or the revolution. Believe me," said the mayor, as though imparting valuable confidential information.

"You mean that Lev Davidovich Bronstein was a fraud? Do you guys still hate Jews here in the former Stalingrad? Didn't any Jews die defending Stalingrad?" I wasn't sure at first that the mayor knew who Bronstein was. But he did.

"Look, you Americans are naive. You don't have Jews hiding behind every door and every tree. We do, or did once, and even today we have to bolt down the furniture to make sure some Bronstein doesn't steal it under our very noses."

"Oh, no, you are the ones who are naive! In America we have millions and millions of Jews. They run the government, control the banks, own the newspapers, manipulate the stock market. They are everywhere. President Reagan is Jewish and so is his wife Nancy. And, would you believe it, I myself am Jewish, on both sides of the family. How do you think I got the job of being President Reagan's very special representative?" That candid explanation terminated the subject of the threat and ubiquitousness of Jews in Russia and America, and the mayor became less informal and much more bearable until he accompanied me and my KGB control, again with motorcycle escort, to the Volgograd airport to catch an early plane.

The plane was full, so the mayor used his authority to have two innocent passengers ejected from the Aeroflot flight to Moscow to make room for the KGB man and the Jewish representative of the Jewish President of the Jewish United States.

The official title of my KGB officer, Geli Neprovsky, was director of the United Nations information center (UNIC) in Moscow.

The UN has had information centers, or UNICs, in all the important capitals of the world. The one in Moscow, by a special arrangement, had to be staffed exclusively by Soviet government officials "seconded" to the United Nations. All were trained KGB intelligence officials, and Geli Neprovsky was yet another high-level KGB operative. The Moscow UNIC was in fact nothing but a center for disseminating Soviet propaganda, casting the UN always in the role of a friend of the Soviet Union and critic of the West, principally the United States. The budding friendship between Russia and America did not permeate UN propaganda aimed at the Russian people. The Soviets were the good guys at the UN and the Americans were always the bad guys.

My first experience with the anti-U.S. and anti-Israeli bias in the overseas operations of the UN Department of Public Information came way before I entered the UN. While still assistant secretary of interior, I was in the Northern Mariana Islands, an eastern extension of Micronesia. At that time the Marianas were part of the Trust Territory of the Pacific Islands, consigned in trust by the United Nations to the United States after World War II. UN radio programs, however, beamed at all of Micronesia (3 million square miles of the Pacific, 97 percent underwater), were the only source of daily news in Saipan, capital of the Marianas. What I heard on those radio programs, in a U.S. territory, was the most amazing condemnation of U.S. policy with emphasis on the wrongness of U.S. support for Israel and the typical PLO line on the situation in the Middle East. This biased content, I later learned, was beamed by the UN throughout the world and disseminated by all the UN information centers, including the one in Washington, D.C.

The influence of the Soviets at the UN in such matters involving public affairs remained curiously anti-American and anti-Israeli well after the U.S.-Soviet confrontation had started to dissipate. The well-established Soviet operatives at the UN remained loyal to their original assignment and continued their Cold War line of propaganda, regardless of the thaw in U.S.-Soviet relations.

As I saw during subsequent trips to the Soviet Union before the fall of the communist regime, the popular TV news program *Vryemia (Time)* featured a UN news segment on a daily basis. Information relayed by the Moscow UNIC gave a totally slanted version of whatever was supposed to be going on at the United Nations. When nothing at all was going on at the United Nations, which was frequently the case, *Vryemia* manufactured something attributed to the Moscow UNIC. The UN news briefs always lauded the Soviets and stuck it to the U.S., Britain, and others of that ilk. "Soviet food and medicine and other forms of humanitarian aid is going to Africa with strong UN support, while America is providing weapons to the entire strife-ridden African continent to promote reactionary regimes and apartheid."

In all fairness, both the Soviet Union and the U.S. were providing weapons to rival East African factions, a corrupt and dangerous practice that has backfired many times. The UN had no influence in preventing this horrendous situation, for neither the U.S. nor the Soviet Union allowed the UN to meddle in such matters. UN-generated Soviet propaganda in Russia was another question. There, the U.S. never protested because the U.S. State Department apparently saw no particular harm in it. The U.S. has an embassy in Moscow equipped with numerous television sets.

Other UNICs around the world were sources of not entirely dissimilar forms of "anti-imperialist" propaganda. The Soviets, with their pervasive influence in the UN Secretariat and within the public affairs department in particular, managed to manipulate the appointment of pivotal Soviet officials to most of the UNICs throughout the world, especially the ones that mattered most.

In Washington, D.C., the UN had an information center headed for a few years by Ms. Phyllis Kaminsky, a Reagan-appointed UN official. She continuously and bitterly complained that one of the Washington UNIC's main responsibilities seemed to be to disseminate to the federal government UN documents put together by the UN PLO representatives to undermine the position of Israel. This was, of course, regarded as an officially sanctioned activity of the UN Secretariat, since the General Assembly had passed the resolution condemning Zionism as a form of racism. Such material was also disseminated to all other UNICs of any significance in the world.

On one of my subsequent trips to the Soviet Union, I was again escorted by the determined Geli Neprovsky in his capacity as "host" and director of the Moscow UNIC. I asked him how it was that TV news programs and newspaper articles in Moscow did not feature the political PLO garbage, unworthy of the UN, that was being disseminated to all other parts of the world via the other UNICs and, of all places, in Washington.

"I thought Jews were not, let us say, well liked in communist Russia, Geli. Why do you censor out PLO propaganda that they get on a regular basis at the Washington UNIC?"

"Well, you must understand that we don't like sneaky Jews in the Soviet Union, but that we Russians also have a little problem with, how you say, Mohammedans," he replied.

"We say Muslims now," I corrected him.

"All right, then Muslims, if you prefer. But you, who have read so much about Russia, surely recall that for three hundred years, give or take, Russians were under the Tartar yoke. Those Tartars were Mongols and Turks who were Muslims, as you say. So we really don't like fancy PLO propaganda."

So, UN information centers throughout the world, financed to a considerable extent by U.S. taxpayers' money, have served for a long period of time (and still do) as anti-Israeli propaganda sources.

The UN Department of Public Information, with massive facilities at its disposal and large quantities of superfluous staff members, is available to members of the General Assembly for distributing documents deemed worthy of UN sponsorship. Massive quantities of PLO anti-Israel propaganda have thus been approved for distribution by the UN Secretariat. After all, a General Assembly resolution then stated categorically that Zionism was a form of racism. No GA resolution had branded anti-Semitism as racism or anything else.

Israel, with a legitimate member state seat in the General Assembly, nevertheless still has no comparable access to the UN Secretariat public information department, whereas UN information centers in all the major world capitals have consistently passed on PLO propaganda to different member state government organs. The PLO has only "observer" status at the UN.

This overt and unashamed misuse of the worldwide facilities of the UN through numerous information centers on all seven continents was certainly not a closely held secret in the days of the Cold War. Very little has changed since then, at least in terms of pro-Palestinian and anti-Israeli material disseminated by the UN. Perhaps there has been an increased degree of subtlety in its presentation, but the manipulation for partisan political reasons of UN information centers throughout the world continues to be an outrage that still seems quite beyond the control of the United States or the interest of members of Congress.

I took other trips to Russia during my last two years in the UN Secretariat. For the next seven years after departing the UN in 1992, as head of the aforementioned institute sponsored by the General Assembly, I continued to do so, although I was no longer known as the "special" representative of Ronald Reagan.

The Institute of East-West Dynamics, a not-for-profit organization, assisted Soviet entities like the largest steel mill in the world, Magnitogorsk (which was also the most inefficient), the province of Murmansk, the Russian Ministry of External Economic Relations, and, indirectly, Mikhail Gorbachev himself. Essentially the work of the institute consisted of teaching American business concepts and technologies to the newly privatized Russian business enterprises. At an official Kremlin dinner in 1992, Gorbachev patted me on the back and said, "Now you are working for me!" Unfortunately, Boris Yeltsin was soon to push him aside.

The tallest government official in the new Russian Federation was a giant (seven-feet, five-inches tall) named Kachanov, who gave a dinner in my honor and asked me in Russian "Kak po-angliski biznesmenny?" or "How do you say *biznesmenny* in English?"

"Businessmen," I replied.

"Ah," he said, "just like in Russian!" I believe he actually thought Americans had adapted that word from the Russian. I let it pass.

Kachanov spoke a little English, of which he seemed quite proud. "It's like what you call 'undertakers,' no?" Finally, I discovered that he had looked up "entrepreneur," a word of French origin, in a French-English dictionary, from which he got "to undertake."

Kachanov warmed up to me, asking the wife of another official sitting next to me to change places with him, and began a more intimate discussion in Russian.

"You know, what you do at this institute to help us is very much appreciated here. I know Gorbachev is interested. But we need to benefit from your honest advice since you are so much more accustomed than we to this new capitalism."

I nodded and listened.

He continued, descending upon me from above, for a good deal of his height was related to his long torso, "You must help us with things that are not always like nuts and bolts. Many new *biznesmenny* are without manners *(byesmanyernyi)*, without principles, they are savage capitalists, well . . . criminals. Most are, of course, Jews. How do you handle that in American business?"

Kachanov was not only disarmingly naive, but refreshingly stupid. I looked up at him, smiled, and said, "Oh, that is no problem in America. We just work hard at converting Jews to Christianity. Christians, as you must be aware, are always guided by the Ten Commandments and adhere to the highest principles of morality."

He blinked several times, then thanked me, and, turning to the lady who had been sitting next to me, asked her to change places with him again.

*   *   *

Geli Neprovsky was still hanging around as director of the UN Information Centre in Moscow during my last trips to Russia. On trips I took after my departure from the UN, I felt it was better to let him hover than to make a scene about having a KGB agent still stalking me and the people I brought with me. In any case, my institute was sponsored by a General Assembly resolution, so, technically, ours was still UN business in Russia. Therefore, everything could still be controlled by the KGB . . . naturally.

Besides, Neprovsky had become, as he put it, a "dear" friend. We had come a long way, he and I.

In my first encounter with him in 1987, still during the Soviet era, he had met me with his chauffeur-driven Mercedes at Vnukovo Airport and literally grunted by way of an initial greeting. That meant "I meet you but do not like you, Ronald Reagan's undercover agent!" On the way to the Rossia Hotel, he asked me if I had had breakfast, and upon my saying I had not, he ordered his driver, a sullen Scandinavian-looking Slav, to stop in front of one of those places they then called "grocery stores" in Moscow, but which could have been called "empty warehouses." They carried almost no groceries and usually refused to sell anything to you, even if they had it in stock.

Geli went in, must have discreetly shown his KGB badge, and soon returned with a piece (half a loaf) of bread and a piece of cold salami. "Here is breakfast!" he said, throwing the offerings at me. It was not an auspicious beginning. But he quickly warmed up to me and became particularly concerned after I snuck out of the Rossia Hotel early one morning at about 7:00 A.M. during that first trip and toured around the Kremlin and other nearby sights by myself, returning to the hotel a little after 10:00 A.M.

Neprovsky was there, having a fit. "Where have you been?" he asked, visibly shaking.

"I took a walk to see the sights," I replied.

"You must never do that alone! You can get hurt," he blurted. I knew he was ashamed I had eluded him.

"Nonsense, Geli! Moscow is full of GAIs [traffic cops], one every block or so. I felt perfectly safe. Besides I have a police badge in my wallet. I struck up a conversation with one of your cops, who was very nice. He admired my badge and showed me his with great pride. I asked him if he would sell it, and he parted with it for about fifty rubles. In fact, I gave him a ten-dollar bill. See, here is the GAI badge!" And lo and behold, I showed Geli the GAI badge I had just purchased. "Zamyechatelno!" Geli exclaimed, meaning "Amazing."

Our relations grew more empathetic up to our last farewell at Vnukovo Airport during my last official visit to Moscow.

"Good-bye, Geli. I hope to see you again soon!"

He seemed to sense a more final farewell and said, "What will happen to us? Will our children and grandchildren ever meet? Will our paths never cross? What is our destiny? What is our fate [sud'ba]? What awaits?"

"Good-bye, Geli," I said and ran for the gate, waving back. After all, we Americans enjoy a derivative English culture that frowns upon quivering upper lips, particularly on KGB agents.

The Cold War finally did come to an end. It collapsed as any absurdity is bound to if it totters around long enough. Communism became a bad word in Russia. Gorbachev, who had brought communism down, then became an even more discredited name. Why? Because he had undermined communism, and now there were bandits in business everywhere, even if most of these new capitalist bandits were former communist officials.

Russia entered a long period of uncertain transition. The trouble was that the process of change was obvious, but it was not clear in what direction the political and social evolution was going. The world seemed to be a slightly better place for the end of big-power confrontation, but the rather abrupt lack of threat of conflict left a dangerous void, a state of uncertainty, the apprehension of chaos and other mysteries that humanity abhors like nature abhors a vacuum.

At the UN, repercussions of the external Russian disorder produced a moderate chaotic effect. UN Secretariat officials from all the former Soviet bloc member states and the former Soviet Union were in danger of becoming orphans. The lack of effective protection from a powerful government made all those concerned feel very disconcerted. Russians began desperately looking around for American, British, French, or even Chinese friends. They needed to get permanent contracts, that is, five-year contracts that carried the tacit renewal guarantee. They needed to safeguard their protracted stays in the U.S. with other sources of income outside the UN to cover their backs just in case.

The UN Secretariat, reflecting, as it was not supposed to, the political situation in the real world, became reorganized over and over again under the incoherent leadership of an Egyptian Copt who spoke French, very imperfect English, and had no idea what the UN Secretariat urgently needed in order to become a more rational international organization. Boutros-Ghali was chosen to succeed Pérez de Cuellar because the newly reconciled superpowers (one "super," the other now rather more "suppressed") continued to agree that the worst thing for the UN would be to have an African secretary-general who was also black. Boutros Boutros-Ghali was African but conveniently white.

Now there was really only one arrogant superpower versus everybody else.

CHAPTER NINE

UN Administrative Chaos

For at least as long as I have been associated and concerned in one way or another with the UN—about twenty years—the Secretariat has been incapable of using the ample funding it receives from member states to help maintain the premises it occupies.

The idea of budgeting ahead for periodic maintenance—something any American homeowner knows is necessary to preserve the value of his property—seems but a theoretical concept at the UN. On the other hand, extravagant expenditures on useless improvements and worthless upgradings are not uncommon manifestations of UN bureaucratic dysfunction, which was made worse by the disappearance of the Cold War tension.

The large UN parking garage, three levels beneath the UN headquarters, once had a fine pavement of gray asphalt, the kind commonly used in the garages of most commercial buildings in New York. Suddenly, parking was shunted from one level to the other as the pavement (thousands of square feet) began to be torn up. At last a new floor for the three levels of parking was completed. The new surface was darker than the perfectly functional asphalt floor that had been there before, but it now had millions of shiny reflecting surfaces. A post hoc explanation was provided for the replacement of the old covering: The shiny "reflectors"—bits of crushed crystalline material—would allow drivers to "see" where the garage floor was and thus prevent accidents. It was left unexplained how looking down at a scintillating pavement while driving could prevent head-on collisions. Today, in any case, road grime and engine oil drippings have covered most of the reflective surfaces.

Another monument to UN administrative frivolity is a gigantic dish antenna thirty feet in diameter equipped with a sophisticated motorized component intended to align it with a communications satellite. By means of this advanced and costly piece of equipment, the UN Secretariat was supposed to maintain direct daily contact with all its overseas information centers—a capability also available through a more primitive device called a telephone.

The need for such instant and secure communications was never established, for UN information centers do not engage in espionage (or should not). Whatever information they may convey to Secretariat headquarters is seldom sensitive to the point of requiring "secure" or instant channels.

The original plan seems to have been to place the impressive dish apparatus off First Avenue in front of the UN building. Objections were raised by a number of member state missions across First Avenue, including the U.S. mission, that such "listening" equipment might be used to violate their security. So the contraption was installed on the river side of the building where it stands today, never having been used. The tall slab of the UN Secretariat building interferes with effective access by the idle dish to any satellite available to date.

At another point in the long record of UN administrative stupidity, new toilet seats equipped with a circular housing for an ultraviolet disinfecting light were installed in some of the restrooms. No credible diseases preventable by such far-fetched forms of sanitation were known to exist in the UN Secretariat at the time. The prevalent rumor was that the costly devices were put in to prevent the spread of AIDS.

The old system for controlling access to the Secretariat building from Forty-second Street had for years functioned without a hitch, since it was simplicity itself. UN staff had entered by one of two gates after flashing a pass with a picture of the bearer. Not long ago a more high-tech entrance system was installed, at high cost, since it involved reconstruction of entrances, new pavement, and significant widening of the passage through the gates. Also involved was an array of parallel turnstiles each equipped with a slot that would read the new magnetized ID cards that were issued. By passing the card through an electronically controlled slot, the turnstile would be released, letting the cardbearer through. However, since the possibility existed that an unauthorized intruder would jump the turnstile, a guard was still kept at each entrance just in case.

Soon the entire system was abandoned and the practice of simply flashing the card reinstated, this time at no cost to U.S. taxpayers who, the reader may recall, actually provide upward of 25 percent of the UN budget. It seems that the turnstiles tended to limit severely the flow of UN employees seeking entrance at midmorning. Most UN staffers arrive at work at the baronial hour of 10:00 or 10:30 A.M. Thus, long lines of what New Yorkers would normally consider very late arrivals began forming on the street outside, exposing to the American public the quaint habits that constitute part of the special UN work ethic.

One of the disturbing aspects of working in the UN Secretariat building is the antiquated and never cleaned air circulation system that recycles stale air throughout the building. The heating system releases large quantities of soot atop the ventilators beneath the windows to the point where leaning over them can result in high dry cleaning bills. This UN soot has a dense, oily quality.

But what really disturbed UN staff members was the presence of asbestos insulation abundantly distributed through the air ducts at a time when that carcinogenic substance was used profusely—the late forties and the fifties. Modern office buildings in New York do not present such problems, and many that are not so modern have conducted inspections to determine and correct the health hazard.

After years of complaining, rebellious UN staffers contacted the New York municipal authorities in charge of controlling the danger posed by flaking asbestos. The city sent an inspector who, somehow, managed to enter the premises, probably by using the visitors' entrance. Once inside, however, the intruder was identified, "arrested" by the

UN guards, kept in a room for two hours without access to a phone, and finally released with the admonition that New York authorities have no jurisdiction in the UN. After all, the UN Secretariat has an infirmary that can diagnose emphysema and the early stages of lung cancer without any violation of the immunity of the international organization.

Expensive tinkering with systems that "ain't broke" masks the fact that normal maintenance (upkeep of elevators, replacement of floor tiles, removal of asbestos from ventilation tubes, repair of bathroom leaks, and the like) is consistently neglected. Maintenance is not budgeted a priori but a posteriori. Once something big breaks, the UN looks to the U.S. Congress to provide the money to fix it during the next appropriation cycle.

That is the case with respect to a strong lobbying effort that has been made by the present secretary-general, Kofi Annan, to convince the Congress that the UN is in a sad state of disrepair and that emergency funds are urgently needed to make things run right. Elevators that stop above or below the floor but no longer level with it need repairing. And how much is needed to upgrade the place? The proposal was for about $2 billion, to be paid immediately.

The most expensive building sold in Manhattan, the GM Building, recently went for $1.4 billion. The entire UN building could be built again for well under $2 billion. Still, repair and refurbishing are activities that involve greater financial opportunities, one would suppose.

A postscript on this chronic administrative hemorrhage is the acquisition of the power plant property adjacent to the UN site on which to build a totally new UN building, since the present one apparently does not meet the high aesthetic specifications required by an international organization. Projected cost of developing the new site with appropriate building or buildings, gardens, and other items of landscaping will be about $7 billion, which the U.S. Congress will in due course be asked to cough up.

Another probable incentive for creating a new UN enclave was the relatively recent rumor that the two UN-rented buildings across First Avenue, DC-1 and DC-2, were to be purchased by an Israeli outfit that was negotiating the sale through the good offices of New York City's Dan Doctoroff, a Jew working for a Jewish mayor. Great alarm spread through the UN that the Israelis might be in a position to influence the UN and even control its finances. The DC-1 and 2 sites have been rented to the UN by something called the UN Development Corporation, a private outfit that has for years rented the two buildings almost entirely to its UN clients.

To illustrate the bizarre relationship between the UN as a tenant and its landlords, let's look into the pathological refusal of UN secretaries-general to control the UN budgetary hemorrhage for midtown Manhattan rentals.

By 1987, I thought I had persuaded Javier Pérez de Cuellar that to placate the non-Jewish Senator Kassebaum in her criticism of the waste at the UN, certain economy-oriented practices might be instituted. Accordingly, I conducted an internal survey with the full cooperation of Undersecretary-General Patricio Ruedas, a Spaniard whose anti-American feelings were tempered by his arrogant disrespect for former Spanish colonials like the secretary-general himself.

Office rental rates in midtown Manhattan were drastically declining by 1987, and landlords everywhere were accepting lease renegotiation rather than lose a tenant altogether. In some cases the mere intimation by the tenant that the economic deflation made it impossible to fulfill the terms of a lease resulted in a voluntary renegotiation.

In the two forty-story towers across First Avenue from the UN Secretariat building, the square foot charges for the UN were way above the average level for other office space in the area, and, as a matter of fact, above the highest levels anywhere in Manhattan. Since the two towers, DC-1 and DC-2, were occupied almost 100 percent by UN offices, without the UN as a tenant, DC-1 and DC-2 would have gone bankrupt at a difficult economic time. Empty buildings that have numerous modifications not made in accordance with the New York City code cannot be rented to anyone. The UN was not required to get permits to gerrymander or rewire any of its offices because the UN is immune from the jurisdiction of the municipal authorities. After careful calculations both with the assistance of the UN administrative personnel in possession of the exact figures and with real estate experts outside the UN, I calculated that a reasonable reduction in square foot rental charges could save the United Nations between $40 and $60 million a year. This was not a bad figure to put before Senator Kassebaum as a token of good faith.

Having completed this somewhat tedious research, I approached the secretary-general. The Spanish undersecretary-general for administration's prior admonition came by way of not-so-subtle sarcasm: "¡Buena suerte!" "Good luck!" he said. "Our boy [meaning the secretary-general] fancies himself an aristocrat because of his fake last name, and claims he will not sully his delicate hands with the administrative grime of such mundane, untidy financial issues."

Somewhat apprehensively, I presented the case to Don Javier. He listened with fingers of both hands touching before him and his glance out the window fixed on the garbage scows transiting below on the East River. When I had finished my exposition of the case, he said: "But why?"

"Why!" I exclaimed. "To save $60 million and keep Senator Kassebaum happy so that she doesn't cut the UN budget by a much larger amount."

"Well," he ventured after an eloquent pause, "we have a contract with the management of DC-1 and DC-2."

I pointed out that I was not suggesting breaking the contract, but that in view of the UN's own "financial strains" (a condition that is chronic at the UN and usually has the credibility of a children's fable) and especially at that juncture with threatened cuts by Senator Kassebaum, the management would see the light quite readily and propose a renegotiated contract since they had two huge buildings on their hands where only the UN could satisfy the description of a suitable tenant.

"But I need to get permission from the General Assembly," Don Javier protested almost inaudibly.

"Did you say the General Assembly?" I asked.

"Yes, the General Assembly, of course," Don Javier repeated with a sparkle in his eye. What a good idea!

"Sir, you do not need permission from the General Assembly or anyone else to perform what is a clear-cut administrative function. Moreover, why would the General Assembly object to getting $60 million that we could reroute to save the chronically starving children in Africa?"

Don Javier's eyes dimmed appreciably and he now mumbled: "Because of the contract we have signed. It was approved by the General Assembly, you see."

"By that same token, Don Javier, you could get a new contract saving the UN millions and bring that before the General Assembly for its enthusiastic approval." My words made him close his eyes and again extend his fingers in a troubled, pensive pose. There were no more garbage scows passing by on the river.

"In any case," I added, "just the effort to renegotiate these outrageously high rentals—even if you met with failure, which I doubt—would reach the receptive ears of Senator Kassebaum and her colleagues in the U.S. Senate. That would make the UN appear like a much more responsible organization in Washington."

The secretary-general looked alarmed and said, "But we are a responsible organization!"

"The standards in Washington are quite different from the norms at the UN, that's all," I said. "But the money the UN gets from the United States is what keeps the UN from going under, so the point of view of Senator Kassebaum merits careful consideration."

The secretary-general again fixed his gaze on the East River and said, "Well, let me think about it." He is probably still thinking about it.

The UN budget could be best described by someone who has a gift for fantasy, like Hans Christian Andersen. But I will continue to do my best.

The publications empire at the UN is so vast, outrageous, and involved that to do it justice would require a second volume. The complicated quadratic equation that regulates what is to be published and in how many languages seems to bear almost no relation to the significance of the material or its anticipated readership. If the objective of this hemorrhage of ink on paper were self-serving publicity, that at least would be an excuse that critics of UN waste could focus on. But that's hardly the case when the UN public affairs department publishes everything in a language that no outsider can or would care to read. Even the identifiable propaganda items, such as those disseminated on behalf of the PLO, are so obtuse as to frequently defy translation. In one case a member of the U.S. mission sitting on the Advisory Committee on Administrative and Budgetary Questions (ACABQ) determined that some of these "documents" cost as much as $750 per page to produce.

There is a total lack of accountability for the allocation of the UN's budget in all its aspects, but particularly with respect to the combined salaries of the UN staff who work in the Secretariat. This lack of accountability makes it possible for many variants of the UN financial wreckage to float ashore in seemingly unrelated waves.

What percentage of the UN budget does the U.S. contribute? In recent times the figure has gone from 25 percent to 18 percent during the Kassebaum cuts, to 20 percent during the financial crisis of the 1990s, back to a theoretical 25 percent, and then to the 22 percent brokered by Richard Holbrooke in December 2000. But these are cosmetic figures that do not take into account voluntary U.S. contributions, enormous tax exemptions that affect the finances of the City of New York, and a number of special funds related to peacekeeping that are assessed independently. The last are used frequently to bail out the UN's administrative and operating costs.

Nor are specifics on these amounts readily available publicly (not in the UN budget contribution passed by Congress); the money is simply urgently required for UN development, human rights activities, or technology improvement. These funds are more basically related to the massive financial fabric the UN has developed over the years for the accomplishment of meaningless and redundant functions, which, if eliminated or simplified, would probably provide the UN with a huge surplus that would allow meaningful expansion of many worthwhile activities for many years to come.

Of course, to admit that the organization has developed chaotically over the years, adding, as we will see, suspiciously redundant operations hidden under inventive and fanciful nomenclature, would be for the UN bureaucracy to agree to commit mass suicide. Bureaucracies are not in business to abolish themselves, but rather to grow ever larger and more complex. It is hard enough to keep the U.S. government within bounds, even if Congress can and does require access to records of most U.S. federal finances in its budgetary oversight capacity. The federal department with the largest aggregate of sensitive or secret information, Defense, is, naturally, the one with the largest budget.

But unlike even Defense, the UN allows no access at all by Congress to any of its records and books. Instead, the UN indirectly provides congressional budget committees with lengthy descriptions of accomplishments and boring accounts of milestones and break-throughs achieved, such as, "The Oil-for-Food Program was the first program in history where the revenues of the country being assisted came from that country itself, Iraq!"* The budgetary requirements and descriptions of UN financial needs are long on the garnish but very, very short on the meat.

This complicated shell game confuses the American press and the U.S. Congress so that one year the UN is believed to be going bankrupt and the next, 2004–5, when the General Assembly approves a basic $3.16 billion budget—representing the largest increase in a decade—its growth, according to the UN, will still be absolutely flat. At the UN it is no different to claim that a budget increase represents flat growth than it is to cry imminent bankruptcy over the years while the UN conducts without difficulty scores of superfluous, nonproductive sinecure activities described earlier in the repeated redundancies in all UN Secretariat departments. The present budget increase has been predicated on the need for additional posts and to modernize and expand UN information technology. Although labeled "flat" at the UN, that, of course, would be seen as growth by most legitimate accounting systems.

The essential facts about the confusing state of the UN budget over the last fifty years are not that difficult to explain. The budget muddle has been the result of the superpowers using the UN to inveigle the rest of the world into believing that it too had a role to play in global affairs. As long as the large mass of outcast semi-independent nations would play the UN game and not interfere with the superpower confrontation

* Benon Sevan's report on the Oil-for-Food Program before the UN Security Council.

during the Cold War, the still-developing pariahs could have access to a forum where they could debate each other ad nauseam and waste as much money as the UN needed in order to elevate it from a sandbox diversion to a world-class theatrical spectacle.

Of course, one of the big drawbacks of having the UN headquarters in New York has been its proximity to Washington, and the large share of UN funding assigned to the United States. That brought in the U.S. Congress, where appearing to save the taxpayers money is always important. The UN was made to order for that congressional pastime. Indeed, the UN has been an extremely wasteful operation, using up large sums with abandon while rejecting any form of meaningful oversight—real waste on which Congress could usefully focus for its own political purposes. The asymmetry of this situation was heightened by the fact that all U.S. contributions, as we have already mentioned, were in hard, convertible currency, whereas the contributions assigned to the Soviet Union and its satellites were in nonconvertible funds, that is silly money, usable only in Eastern Europe. So, in fact, the U.S. was the essential funder of the UN. Of course, the Third World was also, by and large, not paying its assessments because those nations were, after all, poor.

So, early in the Cold War, the fundamental UN financial issue was the U.S. Congress versus the UN. And that easily translated into the U.S. versus the rest of the world at the UN. In those days that confrontation did not seem to matter, for the UN was regarded as a joke by the U.S. government. However, after the collapse of communism, the picture changed radically.

Gradually, the only superpower and the other aspiring inheritors of power in the new world order have begun to delegate significant political issues to the UN. The UN has therefore developed into a lopsided forum with the acknowledgment and consent of the United States—a forum where, for all practical purposes, the world is really aligning itself against the United States.

Was this demonizing of the U.S. a new tendency at the United Nations? Not really. The U.S. Congress for many years had been chastising the UN for its profligate recklessness while the UN (depending on the U.S. as its main benefactor) has been America's main critic.

What this new UN prominence will mean in terms of future world stability and cohesion is not at all a joking matter. For the UN is rapidly becoming a battlefield in which divisive political issues are being presented not in the hope of resolution, but with the prospect of achieving a coalition of the many against the big bully, the rich exploiter, the new imperial power, the United States.

If the United Nations, after being irrelevant for fifty-plus years, becomes a threat to world stability and peace, then that will be the end of the United Nations.

CHAPTER TEN

The UN Culture of Corruption

Soon after my UN appointment in August 1983, an envelope appeared in the mail containing a memorandum that announced that Trident [not their real name] would be the moving company designated to transport my belongings from Washington, D.C., to New York.

The practice in the federal government—conscious as it is of conflicts of interest and congressional oversight—has always been that when an official's goods are transported at government expense, the official must obtain competing quotes from several commercial movers. The government then selects the lowest bid. That at least discourages blatant fraud and theoretically saves the taxpayers money. Not so at the UN.

Trident's agents appeared first at my Interior Department office in Washington and then at my home. They casually assessed the total weight of my entire shipment. They also informed me of the extra expense of packing and unpacking the goods. I pointed out that those charges would be unnecessary since I intended to pack everything myself and also to unpack everything—having experienced previously the happy abandon and careless disregard for order with which some movers pack other people's goods.

Upon their arrival in New York, three days late, the Trident people placed the boxes, furniture, and office equipment inside my new home and told me there would be an extra charge, to be paid on the spot, for weight in excess of the estimate as well as for unpacking. I pointed out that, as their employer, the United Nations would take care of any so-called excess charge and that I intended to do the unpacking myself. The movers intimated that they would not leave without collecting. I intimated, without too much emphasis, that I was in my own house and had a licensed firearm. They left.

Several weeks after settling down in my new home in Westchester and in my new office in Manhattan, facing the East River estuary, a UN functionary of Australian origin appeared in my office unannounced to inform me that I owed Trident a charge for twenty thousand pounds in excess weight and for packing and unpacking the goods I had brought. I replied that I was not aware of the legitimacy of any such claim, which, in any case, the UN had an obligation to pay—all such charges being related to my move. "And," I added, "may I stress that your damn Trident did not perform any packing or unpacking, for which, I would presume, the UN owes Trident nothing." The Aussie left my office suddenly and unexpectedly. I thought he seemed upset.

Next day, again without warning and without even saying "G' day," he burst into my office with another man and blurted, "This is the president of Trident, who wants to talk to you!"

I asked this august personage to take a seat and requested that the UN moving mogul leave us alone. The transportation factotum said no, he would stay.

"You may stay as long as you keep your mouth shut. If you don't, I believe I am fully capable and will be justified in throwing you out."

That took the alleged moving company president aback. Then, without waiting for either of my two "guests" to say anything, I started questioning the president:

- What kind of cozy, crooked deal did his company have with the UN, since the standard procedure in the U.S. government, where I came from, was to get several estimates before choosing a mover?

- What kind of thugs did he have working for him, since they had no idea of the weight of the shipment even after they came to my house and made a vague estimate, had packed nothing, had unpacked nothing as well, and proposed to charge me for both fictitious services?
- Was he aware of the fact that the Interstate Commerce Commission investigated interstate fraud, a federal offense that I was well acquainted with, having moved several times and having served in my U.S. government career in seven federal departments and two White House staffs?
- Was he aware that, in my case, Trident owed me a refund because they were two days late picking up my goods in Washington and three days late delivering them, thus lengthening my hotel stay?

The president of Trident advised the Australian UN official that it was all right to leave us alone. Then he said to me, "Mr. Sanjuan, we have—Trident, that is—a fine furniture store in New Rochelle near where you live. Would you like to stop by at your convenience and pick out any items worth up to fifteen hundred dollars, which we will ship to your home as a token of our appreciation for doing business with you? You, of course, owe us nothing."

A few weeks later, I saw the Australian getting into his car in the UN parking garage not far from where I parked my modest vehicle of vintage American manufacture.

The Australian let himself into a contemporary model BMW Bavaria, the most expensive car available from that company at the time. It figured.

It was rather obvious that Trident, in order to do business with the UN, had to pay this corrupt UN official on the side.

That episode gave me an early taste of the comfortable moral informality that prevailed throughout the UN organization. But it was a mere initiation.

What surprised me more than anything else during these early stages was that, accompanying numerous unorthodox and even unethical practices, there prevailed a lighthearted spirit of openness and acceptance. There was clearly an "international" code of behavior that placed UN officials above the traditional rules. It was sort of like saying, "No, we are not rascals, we are international civil servants," an important distinction not easily perceived by outsiders.

As already described, the tolerance of a sizable Soviet intelligence collection operation was, to say the least, an enormous conflict of interest. What, therefore, would restrain—in such a quaint political culture—the conflict involving individuals favoring special elements of the private sector of a member state? Private sector conflicts of interest have been and are rampant among UN employees, burdened as they are with only light housekeeping duties—a bloated staff composed largely of supernumeraries. UN staffers have been conducting improper personal business during office hours with total impunity since the beginning of UN time.

Nepotism has been and is widespread, the boldest and most famous examples of which related to Kurt Waldheim, who hired his nieces at the lowest clerical level and soon had them promoted to the highest level of the international civil service—director status. Waldheim subsequently became the first elected president of his native country who would not be granted a visa to come to the United States because of his World War II criminal background. Waldheim certainly had an enormous conflict when he assumed the position of UN secretary-general. UN secretaries-general should be the antithesis of war criminals. Surely that is an easy concept to grasp.

The U.S. government has possessed detailed foreknowledge of the background of all the individuals it has supported for the position of secretary-general, including Waldheim. Similarly, the U.S. government understood perfectly well the conflict that Mr. Connor, a former CEO of Pricewaterhouse, would have after becoming UN undersecretary-general for administration.

The support of an American for this sensitive position was justified in the Clinton White House in the following manner: The position was to be ostensibly reserved for an American so that the U.S. could pretend to oversee the wise husbanding of the large U.S. contribution to the UN budget. The U.S. Congress, of course, had no say in confirming the appointment of any American to the UN Secretariat ostensibly made by a UN secretary-general, albeit actually by the president of the United States. However, if the secretary-general, who then was Boutros Boutros-Ghali, had refused to agree, he would have been easily browbeaten by the president of the only remaining superpower.

During his early tenure as undersecretary-general for administration, Mr. Connor, apparently oblivious to his conflict of interest image, was credited with approving numerous additional UN contracts for Pricewaterhouse. Perhaps it was a mere coincidence that the firm was also repeatedly introduced as the preferred accountant to new Central Asian UN member states seeking urgent assistance from UN economic aid agencies. To qualify for aid from the UN Development Programme (with two m's), these countries needed evidence of modern five- and ten-year economic plans and income and budget projections. Pricewaterhouse accountants were ready to conduct such studies for very high professional fees.

Prior to the appointment of Mr. Connor by the Clinton White House, the first Bush administration had asked former U.S. attorney general Richard Thornburgh in 1990 to be the UN undersecretary-general for administration under the newly appointed Boutros Boutros-Ghali. Thornburgh and I had some interesting conversations prior to my departure from the UN Secretariat, during which I tried to precondition him to the relaxed ethical standards in the UN and to the remaining Soviet intelligence-collecting apparatus in the Secretariat.

During a period of two years, Thornburgh conducted a very intensive investigation and came out with a very critical, one might even say damning, report. The report, of course, was an internal UN document, and clandestine negotiations resulted in Thornburgh's departure, after which he pursued a more satisfying career as a Washington lawyer. He was followed by an American woman who had senior diplomatic experience, Melissa Welles.

A mutual friend of Mrs. Welles and mine recommended that she talk to me, and we began a series of meetings during which I did for her what I had tried to do for Thornburgh. Soon, after an episode with a Canadian aircraft firm whose outrageously overpriced UN contract was supposed to be accepted without bidding, Melissa Welles said to me that she was appalled at the corruption that prevailed in all outside business deals involving the UN Secretariat. Melissa Welles was also eased out prematurely because she tried to institute the practice of open bidding at the UN, and she did not agree to comply with the specially corrupt terms of the UN system.

With its far-flung offices and program activities all over the world, the UN travel budget is enormous—on the order of $1 billion a year. The contract for providing travel services is therefore very lucrative, and competition among private booking agencies to handle it is stiff—or ought to be.

In 1986, shortly after his victory in New York's U.S. Senate race, a business friend of Al D'Amato's, the head of the Fugazy Travel Agency, made a bid for the contract to handle all travel at the UN. Since UN custom dictated that such a bid be accompanied by a large monetary offer, Fugazy agreed to pay the UN Secretariat $850,000. Another outfit, Dawn Travel, offered $250,000, and still another put up $500,000.

The UN Secretariat, after discussions with all three bidders, granted the contract to Dawn Travel. This in spite of the fact that Dawn was the least experienced firm and had prefaced their offer not only with the lowest monetary inducement but also with a number of peculiar conditions. One of those was that normal travel arrangements for UN officials would be paid three months in advance, with the tickets to be made available to the traveler only the day before his departure. That seemed to provide Dawn with a very large revolving fund that could be lent on a short-term basis at the normally high short-term loan interest rates. These facts raise the question of whether there may have been kickbacks to UN officials who continued to profit from the arrangement.

Fugazy Travel naturally felt that something dishonorable had occurred and petitioned Senator D'Amato. D'Amato called the UN undersecretary-general for administration and was told that the UN did

not care a fig what his constituent felt or did not feel. The UN was beyond the jurisdiction of a U.S. senator, and the senator could stick it if
he did not like it.

That Senator D'Amato was at the time chairman of a Senate committee did not in any way affect the UN's handling of his inquiry.

Perhaps one of the most idiosyncratic departures from universally
accepted bureaucratic practice is the custom at the UN for officials involved with personnel issues to solicit sexual favors from women employees—and not only from women at the clerical level. The usual
sequence of events has involved any heterosexual administrator interested in satisfying his normal urges with whatever moderately attractive
female has been due for a raise in grade. Actual advancement following
eligibility for promotion at the UN can occur either rapidly (for example, Secretary-General Waldheim's relatives brought into the UN at the
lower clerical grades were rapidly elevated to director levels) or otherwise
after painfully slow and unexplained circumspection during repeated
contract renewals for UN staff members in the professional ranks who
may lack obvious political clout. Secretaries (general staff) are hired on
a one-year trial basis, after which they are anointed as permanent. But
grade promotions for general staff are something else that may take several lifetimes to accomplish.

My first exposure to the generally accepted practice of sexual harassment came about six months after my arrival. An attractive, moderately
young woman at the professional three level was recommended by her
boss in my division, who was supposed to be my principal political affairs officer although I did not allow him, a former high official in the
Warsaw communist apparatus, to perform any such functions for me.

I approved the Pole's recommendation for the promotion of his subordinate, however. A few weeks after I had taken that action, the woman
to be promoted came to me and complained that an assistant director
in the office of the secretary-general, apparently in charge of expediting
such promotions, had suggested a tryst or two to her as a way to expedite the paperwork.

I called the assistant director in question to my office and confronted him. Rather than denying the accusation, the assistant director informed me that there was nothing unusual about a request for sex on the assistant director's part in order for him to move along the request for promotion.

I brought this bizarre farce to the attention of the special assistant to the secretary-general, the already mentioned Olivares, who told me that the assistant director was driven by testosterone, a normal heterosexual condition, so there was nothing extraordinary about the whole matter.

In fact, sexual harassment as such did not officially exist at the UN Secretariat because it was not recognized as a deviation from accepted normal practice.

Only the more outrageous impositions on sexually desirable women occasionally led to flare-ups and ultimately to a scandal or two. In the early 1990s, the undersecretary-general for administration and management, an Argentine named Luis María Gómez, imposed his service requirements so blatantly and physically on his female coordinator for panel of counsel [sic] that she, Ms. Catherine Claxton, repeatedly abused, harassed, and physically injured, sought legal advice outside the UN. The threatened suit would have been rejected by any U.S. court due to the immunity enjoyed and abused by her tormentor, but the mounting adverse publicity in New York reached such a level that Ms. Claxton was found by an internal disciplinary board to have been victimized and was awarded a large cash indemnification. Gómez, who continued to pursue his outrageously high-handed tribal folkways, ultimately resigned from the UN and returned to the pampas.

It was interesting that the Gómez episode—Ms. Claxton's vindication and his ultimate resignation—was regarded by most people at the UN with whom I spoke at the time as an outrageous development not insofar as his behavior was concerned, but with regard to the unusual outcome of what was really no big deal.

Such matters are clearly not considered to be as serious at the UN as they are in Europe, the United States, or Canada because the UN is "an international arena." The rights of women are therefore treated with the benevolent disregard that makes the organization a more comfortable environment for members of male-oriented societies outside the realm of what is called "Western" civilization, a term that usually includes both Argentina and the Netherlands.

Thus it may be hard to appreciate why a former Dutch prime minister, burdened with an excess of testosterone even at the reasonably mature age of sixty-five, escaped censure by Kofi Annan after being found guilty of improper conduct by the UN's usually docile Office of Internal Oversight Services. Mr. Rudd Lubbers, until recently high commissioner for refugees (a majority of them women, by the way), has been alleged to have repeatedly squeezed the buttock of a fifty-one-year-old woman working for him who finally charged him with sexual harassment. The verdict was revised by Kofi Annan as not sustainable. Mr. Lubbers maintained that his actions were but a "friendly gesture," something that, although not accepted in the Netherlands, is understood and tolerated at the UN.

Corruption at the UN began at the top and continued at the level of all the UN secretaries-general after the death of Dag Hammarskjöld. Burmese secretary-general U Thant practiced a massive form of cronyism, bringing into his administration a steady influx of South Asian supernumeraries. New offices and departments had to be invented to accommodate his crony hangers-on who had bloated the office of the secretary-general beyond all foreseeable expectations.

U Thant's successor Kurt Waldheim, as we have already noted, brought into the Secretariat nieces and other relatives who had no professional qualifications, but whom he made arrangements to promote to the top professional levels. But that "scandal" was regarded at the UN as a mere idiosyncrasy, and the details were passed around in the form of a series of fairly clever Austrian jokes about Waldheim's foibles.

The most famous of these anecdotes was that Waldheim in his youth did not belong to the Hitlerjugend because he was a real Nazi, but because he enjoyed riding horseback, available through Hitlerjugend clubs. So Waldheim was not a Nazi, but the horse he rode was a Nazi.

Javier Pérez de Cuellar prided himself on not being involved in the blatant corruption that he admitted prevailed in the UN. As he was fond of saying, "Yo no soy de esta casa" ["I am not of this house"]. By that he implied that the corruption of the institution he managed was none of his business. All administrative matters were, in fact, outside his purview for he was a diplomat and an internationalist "thinker." He held on to such sincere conceits in spite of the fact that during his two five-year terms he did not conceive a single memorable idea or initiative in the field of international relations. I pointed out to him on one occasion, in mock exasperation, that he should have paid rent for occupying a large office in an organization he claimed to not be involved with. However, his studied detachment did not exclude bringing his Peruvian cronies into positions of strong influence at the top of the UN ladder. One of them qualified for an executive UN position because he had once worked at Bloomingdale's.

Boutros Boutros-Ghali kept the venerable tradition of cronyism alive and well. He favored his brother-in-law, a certain Fred Nadler, who set up a front company called Euroswiss Syndicators (figure that one out!) at 110 East Fifty-seventh Street in New York. Nadler in fact helped expedite a large number of UN contracts involving the U.S. private sector and took well-earned fees, since he was worth his weight in gold for providing ready access to all UN procurement offices as the brother-in-law of the big man.

A year after leaving the Secretariat, I received a visit in my new office a few blocks from the UN from a top official working in the Secretariat department that deals with disarmament affairs. He was a former Soviet intelligence officer (military) now schlepping as an orphaned UN civil servant after the fall of the Soviet Union. This character praised me for the "great work" I was doing trying to bring the new Russia and its new friend, America, closer together. Then he added that he knew I had contacts with important American banks and business interests—unfortunately an exaggeration. Finally he came to the point.

An associate of his in Moscow with friends in Kiev, capital of the Ukraine, had access to large quantities of Russian shotguns, reputedly the best in the world, for Russians like to hunt, and they have an excellent small-arms industry witnessed by the worldwide proliferation of

AK-47s. Could I help in finding a market for these items in the United States?

I headed a not-for-profit, tax-exempt institute created with UN endorsement in the form of a United Nations General Assembly resolution (46–15 of 1989), passed at the request of both the Soviet Union and the United States. Its objective was well known at the UN—to facilitate better understanding between the United States and the former Soviet bloc countries in developing trade and investment ties by creating, in Russia and Eastern Europe, institutions like federal reserve banks, stock exchanges, development banks, chambers of commerce, and the like—not by selling shotguns!

I told my Russian visitor from the UN Secretariat disarmament department that I deplored the proliferation of arms of any caliber, that I didn't know anybody in the shotgun business, and that I was appalled that he, who was in the disarmament business, should be peddling guns when he already received an excellent salary paid in large part by U.S. taxpayers.

Nothing daunted, the same individual popped by my office a month later.

"This time I have something big and worthy of somebody of your standing," he said.

I dreaded the thought of what he might say next, and with good reason.

"I have beryllium—you know, the metal that is so useful when making nuclear bombs—forty thousand tons of it sitting in railroad freight cars in Kazakhstan. It is for sale. There must be some broker you know who wants to get his hands on what is practically a controlled substance."

This time I skipped the sermon and told him I would "look into it." As soon as he had left my office with a satisfied look on his face, I called an FBI agent whom I still referred to by the code name of Mason. I told him the beryllium story. The shotgun business I had thought too trivial to relay.

Mason told me that sales of controlled substances were under the purview of special investigators from the U.S. Department of Commerce. Mason would relay my information with an urgent sticker on it to his counterpart in Commerce.

A few days later I received a call from somebody who was a special investigator from Commerce. I told him the story all over again.

"Well, Commerce doesn't buy beryllium anymore, so I don't know what to say," he replied.

"You miss the point! This is about a UN official trying to sell an illegal, nuclear weapons component in the United States. I don't want anyone, not even Commerce, to buy it. It is the illegal activity that I am concerned with. You understand?"

"Well," said the less-than-bright Commerce investigator, "we don't investigate activities at the UN. That would be the FBI."

This anecdote is one of many more I could offer. They poignantly illustrate how the UN Secretariat is a convenient shelter for an extensive Lavender Hill mob that has been and is beyond the reach of the law—anybody's law.

Soviet undersecretary-general Vassily Safronchuk, the vain and indiscreet former Red Army artillery captain, soon developed close friendships with members of the Russian Brooklyn mafia, several of whom found a base of operations in his office. The capo of this group was shot by mafia rivals after entering his New York apartment building, while still in the lobby talking to his wife on the intercom. Curiously enough, extortionist elements in the Russian mafia obtained detailed information about the addresses and daily habits of other Russians at the UN and contacted them, using primitive but effective bribery threats such as "You pay us three hundred dollars every month or we will shoot a member of your family." Several of these hapless victims ran to my office, now outside the UN, but only two blocks away, asking for help. Fortunately, my live contacts with the FBI led to wiretaps, willingly accepted by the Russian UN victims of Safronchuk's mafia buddies, and to the cessation of the extortion attempts.

A strikingly patriarchal-looking Sudanese member of Safronchuk's senior staff ran not only one crime-connected smuggling enterprise in New York, taking advantage of his Sudanese UN mission brothers who had diplomatic immunity, but in addition coordinated an internal ring of drug distributors. This Sudanese patriarch, who sported a beard that made him look like King Xerxes of Persia, met an unfortunate end while recovering from an operation in a New York hospital. He was thrown off a fire escape.

Are such examples of illegal activity triggered by an abundance of opportunities found only in New York, the city of sin? Hardly. UN corruption is systemic and worldwide.

For example, the long arm of the Yakuza, the mafia of Japan, long ago wrapped itself around the UN Secretariat.

Ryoichi Sasakawa, well known in Japan and internationally as one of the biggest Yakuza crime figures, was advised by an agent of his who was the head of a UN-accredited nongovernmental organization that there was a way for Sasakawa to achieve greater positive recognition. He should donate millions to the World Health Organization. Sasakawa the gangster could thus mutate into Sasakawa the hero.

Sasakawa's earliest connection with the UN had been through his good friend Bradford Morse, former U.S. congressman and durable head of the United Nations Development Programme.

Sasakawa had reached that stage (that John Gotti, a much nattier dresser, was prevented from even approaching) when pure self-aggrandizement became his new goal in life. Of course, he still dealt with anything that would turn a profit, like controlling with an iron fist Japan's drug distribution system, including illegal narcotics (publicly condemned by the World Health Organization), and strangling Japanese consumers with unconscionably high prices, all while getting his picture taken with children to promote his "nice old man" image. A touching porcelain memento was distributed at the UN during the initial stages of Sasakawa's transfiguration. It was a small statue of Sasakawa carrying his mother on his back up to the top of Mount Fuji.

There is a bust of Sasakawa at the UN in honor of his great human-itarian contributions.

But this is small potatoes compared to the extensive and systematic corruption engaged in by the UN Secretariat and UN agencies in foreign countries. Consider, for example, the testimony of Conrad B. Stergas, an American aviation safety inspector who for years worked for major American airlines. The UN Office of Aviation Safety and Flight Standards hired Mr. Stergas as a consultant in 1994. But that office was abolished shortly after Mr. Stergas began to complain about the intolerable situation in East Africa.

Mr. Stergas came to me after being referred by Washington think tank investigators doing research on the UN. I in turn put him in touch with Robert Erlanger, a New York criminal lawyer who had a reputation for fighting institutional corruption on behalf of abused victims. Stergas produced a detailed account about the UN in East Africa.

Stergas said that in March 1994, he had accepted a job with the newly created Office of Aviation Safety and Flight Standards at the United Nations. He had great expectations of providing assistance to the world organization.

His job was to oversee aviation regulatory compliance and aircraft utilization matters for the UN's fleet of chartered aircraft used in the United Nations Operation in Somalia (UNOSOM). The cost of running this fleet was about $100 million annually—one-quarter of which was U.S. taxpayers' money. Stergas was the first person sent by the UN to observe and advise on aviation matters on a full-time basis in the UN operation in East Africa, which comprised Djibouti, Somalia, and Kenya.

During briefings in New York before Stergas's departure, the UN office told him that he might meet some resistance in accomplishing his job. From his thirty years of experience in aviation, he understood this to mean possible disputes over regulatory matters.

Apparently nobody could prepare him for what followed.

On the day of Stergas's arrival in Nairobi, Kenya, at the UNOSOM office, at 3:00 A.M., he was unceremoniously hustled off to a twenty-dollar-a-night hotel room that the UN had reserved for him in a dangerous part of town. Although there were twenty-five UN-approved hotels in town, the UN booked Stergas into a fleabag that was far below the UN's own security standards. Within a few minutes of his arrival at the registration desk, as if on cue, four men came into the hotel lobby, toting pistols and a machine gun. Referring to Stergas, they were yelling to one another: "Shoot this one, shoot this one!" They robbed Stergas of almost everything, including his U.S. passport. He immediately reported the robbery to UN headquarters in New York.

A few days later, while Stergas was trying to complete preparations to replace needed personal effects, a ranking UN official in Nairobi walked up to him and said: "You have too many pens in your pocket. Wait until you get to Mogadishu, you'll get two bullet holes in the head." The UN official was obviously implying that Stergas would be assassinated because of his reporting on aviation matters.

He also relayed this incident to UN headquarters in New York and requested that they provide him most urgently "with instructions on how to proceed." For twenty-seven days UN headquarters made no reply to more than twelve requests from Stergas for instructions. Finally they asked him to return to New York. A few days after doing so, Stergas submitted a report describing conditions in East Africa. Three days later the UN terminated his employment contract under the pretext of "frustration of purpose."

His personal experience was significant because of the opportunity he had, while waiting in Nairobi, to discover how UN peacekeeping operations were run in East Africa.

Stergas was originally recommended to the UN by an aviation colleague who had ties to persons of responsibility within the aviation industry in East Africa. He met many of these people, who lived in fear for their lives not only from threats by crooked agents, brokers, and local government officials, but also from the complicity of equally corrupt UN officials in the field and at UN headquarters.

"My aviation sources in Africa were reporting such dangerous deficiencies as the UN doing business with providers of critically substandard aviation equipment and the UN's undermining its own bidding process that had been designed to insure the acquisition of safe aircraft at a reasonable commercial price," said Stergas. These shady practices put at risk the life of any person who traveled on UN aircraft in East Africa. Added to this, the UN had no aviation safety program or guidelines, but relied on this policy: "If it crashes, we'll just get another one." Stergas's aviation sources said that the object seemed to be one of "move a lot of tonnage and look good for the aid donors." The crashes did not count. Although corruption was an important factor, as Stergas's aviation sources said, "It is UN incompetence, negligence, and arrogance that have an equally if not greater negative effect on the UN's performance."

A large number of fraudulent foreign brokers of aircraft—aircraft being one of the largest UN budget items—obtained Kenyan brokers' licenses in collusion with corrupt UN officials who had local connections. These "licensed" brokers were in a position to lease decrepit aircraft procured through chains of disreputable "brokers" for UN operations in East Africa. "For example, a U.S. hustler of near wrecks leases an aircraft to an operator in Zimbabwe who in turn leases it to a 'licensed agent' in Nairobi who in turn leases the aircraft to the UN. A near hulk that originally sells for $40,000 winds up in Nairobi renting to the UN at rates equivalent to those of well-equipped aircraft worth several million. Everybody makes a profit, most especially the UN procurement officer at the end of the chain," recounted Stergas.

The corruption did not stop at the UN's traffic in unairworthy aircraft.

Aviation sources in Nairobi reported to Stergas such continued flagrant abuses as the issuing of bids for rental contracts at 4:00 P.M. with a deadline of 4:05 P.M. on the same day to guarantee sweetheart deals already agreed upon before the bids were issued. One particular $10 million scam involved changing tendered documents in favor of another company. Aviation sources could not understand why the UN person involved in the scam was still working for the UN after his complicity was proven. Stergas's sources said that they could "put together a very powerful team of witnesses who were fed up with the UN corruption."

"I was introduced to persons in responsible positions who were documenting corruption at the UN and who knew of some honest persons in high level UN positions keeping diaries of such events in the hope that one day soon an investigation would be instituted to look into the mess in East Africa. For example, I have been told of the UN practice of establishing phony UN offices, fraudulent staff manipulations and of over-ordering supplies to the extent that many UN stocks in East Africa are more than four years old." In addition, large quantities of useless, expired medicines were purchased and continuously stocked, a threat to everyone's health. UN vehicles were procured for use by relatives of local UN officials. Particularly profitable was the practice of producing phony aviation fuel invoices, an activity that required constant involvement by UN officials, as did the fabrication of bogus nongovernmental organizations invented to receive shipments ordered in their name.

"I have been told that in Mogadishu every trick is used by UN officials to over-purchase." From Mombasa to Mogadishu, shipments were made at three times the normal tariff rate. In East Africa, "godfathers" protected UN procurement officers. Stergas's sources believed that in the previous four years, something in the range of $500 million had been lost to crooks in East Africa through UN operations.

Some of what Stergas discovered was confirmed by Karl Paschke, the United Nations inspector general and head of the Office of Internal Oversight Services. In a report on East Africa, he said that management in Nairobi, Kenya, was so bad that to allow it to continue "would be reprehensible." A UN spokesman, Fred Eckhard, said that Secretary-General Kofi Annan "concurs with the findings."

But nothing was done and the mismanagement continued undisturbed.

Later, the UN Office of Internal Oversight Services (OIOS) in New York identified another corrupt and very lucrative aircraft contract–bidding practice. A particular contractor had been submitting multiple bids in the name of various companies; however, all of the bids related to the same contractor. The UN would then simply select the contractor's lowest bid, which was in fact a high bid. A source at the UN in New York said, "The UN covers this up. None of the OIOS reports get published concerning this type of issue. The UN overtly allows this contractor to continue corrupt practices." As a result of investigations in 1993, this particular contractor was supposedly prohibited from being involved in future UN contracts. But nothing, in fact, happened.

Robert Albracht, an aviation expert contracted in 1993 to oversee UN aviation operations in East Africa, said to Stergas, "The corruption was blatant. Although a particular contractor was banned from being involved in UN contracts, I saw the contractor still behind the scenes paying employees under the name of another company and otherwise still very much a presence and involved."

"These practices cannot be allowed to continue under any pretense of UN reform," Stergas observed.

"The system of corruption at the UN needs to be exposed and stopped for perfectly obvious reasons, one of which is that U.S. taxpayers are footing a bill of close to $200 million in order to subsidize crooks in East Africa." The corruption got out of hand when Boutros-Ghali was secretary-general.

"It is now Kofi Annan's job to clean up the mess," Stergas stated in his very candid report.

Secretary-General Kofi Annan subsequently announced a "saving" of $200 million in UN operations, which he planned not to return to donor states but to use in aid of the kind supplied to East Africa. The UN was saving money in New York to subsidize criminals overseas.

An account of all these criminal activities was written by Conrad Stergas in 1996 and presented to the UN Secretariat that same year. No action has been taken on it to date. The UN is immune from the jurisdiction of courts in the United States. After turning in his report, Mr. Stergas was immediately fired in spite of having a valid contract. No compensation was made for his losses in Africa.

If the entire East African operation has been so thoroughly compromising, if United Nations information centers are used as national propaganda distribution outlets, if UN agencies like UNESCO have been totally co-opted by anti-Israeli and anti-American political elements contrary to the basic rules of neutrality that are supposed to control all UN activities, if organized criminal elements have permeated the UN Secretariat in New York—what can be expected of UN activities in other parts of the world?

CHAPTER ELEVEN

Shady Characters

ecause the UN Secretariat is by nature an eclectic organization, it is not surprising that its upper-level staff should consist of people who have esoteric backgrounds. A provincial American might react to this by making an invidious comparison between the way American functionaries understand the responsibilities of public service and the way foreign panjandrums take advantage of the self-help opportunities provided by the highest echelons of the UN Secretariat.

Such a narrow view is not sustainable when one looks at the collective UN biographic panorama through the wide-angle lens preferred at the United Nations. That the advantage-takers are multinational befits the ethos of an international organization. They are Africans, Americans, Cypriots, Pakistanis, and members of many other nationalities.

Let us take the fascinating history of Mr. Iqbal S. Riza, until recently UN *chef de cabinet* or chief of staff, the right-hand man of UN Secretary-General Kofi Annan. Different versions and facets of his identity appear, when seen in the aggregate, like a portrait by Braque or Picasso in his early cubist period. Mr. Riza resigned under a cloud, according to the *New York Sun,* in December 2004. He was soon thereafter rehired at the undersecretary-general level to advise the UN on cultural matters.

A Pakistani national, Mr. Riza came to the United Nations Secretariat from the Pakistani foreign service. During the Iran-Iraq war, he acted in a UN observer capacity, but a persistent allegation of serious impropriety brought him back to UN headquarters in New York. The allegation involved Iqbal's sale of American intelligence photographs of the Iraqi front to Iranian authorities for a figure that, depending on the accounts, varied from $40,000 to $75,000, but which was entered into his personal record as $60,000.

The controversy brought Iqbal physically back to the Office of Legal Affairs in New York, where he was confined to a small cubbyhole without his name being listed in the UN telephone directory, even in the alphabetical register. That amounts to very strong punishment at the UN.

Somewhat concerned that such a sentence of exile was being carried out in a space contiguous with some of the offices in my division, I asked the legal counsel, a certain Carl-August Fleischhauer, about the real significance of Iqbal's exile. Fleischhauer, whose legal pomposity was reinforced by a vulnerable Teutonic sense of self-importance, replied, "I don't want to talk about it at all! Do you understand?"

"No, I don't understand," I replied.

"Well, ask your friend, the secretary-general," Carl-August caterwauled as he suddenly rushed down the hall, pretending to look for an elevator.

After a cooling-off period, Iqbal was sent on another mission, this time to Central America. There are several vague and murky versions of what Iqbal did there, but nothing that runs by with a long enough tail to grab except that he informed the UN secretary-general of impending "plans" by the U.S. government to invade Nicaragua.

Next, Iqbal was posted in the UN Department of Disarmament Affairs, where Kofi Annan was in charge as undersecretary-general. The two men became close friends.

Some time later, Iqbal Riza was appointed UN Secretariat chief of staff by Kofi Annan. This reaffirmed my suspicion that rumors and misunderstandings about Iqbal over the years had been precisely that—rumors and misunderstandings—a product of the unfortunate lack of awareness outside sophisticated UN circles as to what actually goes on inside the UN. It is a complex arena of negotiations and compromises that are quite beyond the pale of ordinary people's experiences and the conventional American supermarket morality.

In late December 2004, Iqbal Riza resigned abruptly as chief of staff. Rumors in the newspapers (the *New York Times,* among others) indicated that he had been asked to leave by Kofi Annan at the insistence of the U.S. State Department in view of the mounting pressure from the U.S. Congress over the Oil-for-Food scandal. The pressure was on Kofi to clean up various elements on his staff. Riza denied being asked to leave, alleging that UN retirement age requirements had brought about his departure. Riza was seventy years old. Retirement age at the UN is sixty-two.

*   *   *

The fall of the Soviet empire was a momentous event in modern history. It ended the Cold War and presaged the debut of America's world empire.

Well, not quite. Certainly not at the UN.

After the collapse of the USSR, the justifiably panicky KGB and GRU Soviet types in the UN Secretariat regrouped, after satisfying themselves that they would not be shipped back to Moscow and other parts of Russia en masse. They were still part of the UN Russian elite and easily managed to regain control over other Russian staff members, to the detriment of those who had foolishly decided to express overtly their tender, sincere feelings for newfound American friends and American values.

UN headquarters in New York is located in the midst of an urban environment that is regarded as culturally corrosive by many UN hypocrites, the epicenter of the most extreme excesses of the American ethos. It was altogether natural, therefore, that some conscientious Russians, such as Vadim Perfiliev, should decide to purge the Secretariat of those compatriots who now appeared to be even moderately critical of the Soviet past.

Vadim Perfiliev had a most remarkable personal history. He was expelled from France in 1985 as a KGB agent while serving in Paris as a Soviet "diplomat." In the chronology of careers as fascinating as Perfiliev's, there are understandably mysterious, safeguarded intervals, or lacunae. Such appears to have been his next assignment. After that blank episode, Perfiliev joined the United Nations Secretariat in 1991 as part of the Soviet UN Secretariat quota, still seconded by the now moribund USSR government.

The layperson may ask at this point how it was that a UN secretary-general could accept a Russian on his staff who had a proven record as a KGB operative previously made public by the French government. The answer to that is easy. Remember that UN secretaries-general accepted Soviet officials to work on the UN Secretariat staff based only on a two-page form submitted pro forma by the Soviet government. After two or three years, the seconded staffers were expected to return to the Soviet bureaucracy. The secretary-general, of course, would have no right to interfere with a Soviet secondment request—which was a request only in the diplomatic sense of the word. In fact, the submission of a Soviet official's name had been regarded all along as tantamount to a demand.

The layperson might also ask why at that time there were still no Israeli UN Secretariat staff members, when, in principle at least, Israel was allotted a minimum of fifteen positions as its quota. That is also easy to answer. Israel had no secondment arrangement.

In 1991, Perfiliev went to work in the UN Department of Public Information, but his sojourn there was short. He was removed at the request of his boss, the previously mentioned Thérèse Sevigny, who found his performance poor and involving a "parallel agenda."

Perfiliev was next appointed political adviser to the special representative of the secretary-general to Mozambique. That representative was a man of Italian nationality named Aldo Romano Ajello. Perfiliev was soon removed from that position after Mr. Ajello caught him copying confidential files from Ajello's computer.

Consistency has always been rewarded in the Soviet Union. So, at the insistence of the USSR, Perfiliev was not fired but instead got reappointed to the office of the United Nations special representative to Angola, where (alas!) he was again noticed clumsily tampering with the computer files of his supervisor. As a result, Perfiliev was removed from Angola and, again at the insistence of the all-but-defunct USSR, appointed to the position of director in the newly reorganized UN Political Department at headquarters in New York.

Perfiliev's next supervisors, succeeding each other in the political department, were Undersecretary-General Goulding and Undersecretary-General Prendergast (both Brits), who both repeatedly requested that Perfiliev's contract with the United Nations not be renewed. Notwithstanding their recommendations, and after considerable pressure exerted by the Russians on Secretary-General Boutros-Ghali—who was then lobbying for another five-year term and needed every vote he could get in the Security Council—Perfiliev was transferred to the General Assembly department. That department was headed by Undersecretary-General Jin of China, who extended Perfiliev's contract.

So the problem was solved!

The United Nations Secretariat is a minimal working environment where upward mobility is provided to those who pursue well-defined career goals along with the necessary support of their sponsoring member states. This would appear to contradict the views of some, like former New York mayor Ed Koch, who, as mentioned earlier, called the UN a "stagnant cesspool." Certainly Perfiliev's progress was proof of the opportunities that are open to all at the UN who strive upward with the proper backing.

During 1995, Perfiliev, now feeling much more secure, revived an almost nostalgic Soviet-era theme. For this he could not be held morally accountable since he was still, vaguely, a seconded Soviet UN official, having entered the UN during the waning years of the Soviet Union. Accordingly, he began to depict the secretary-general's belated proposals for UN reform—for example, Boutros-Ghali's efforts to cozy up to the U.S. in order to win reappointment—as being contrary to the interests of the Third World. Perfiliev contended that the secretary-general was "the man of Washington" and that his reform plan was aimed at converting the United Nations into a "branch of the Department of State." Such statements incited mistrust and generated lack of confidence in Boutros-Ghali's putative reform program among some eighty UN member states and also provoked widespread opposition to American pressure for reform. Two important UN committees—the Fourth Committee and the Special Committee of 24—soon opposed the secretary-general's restructuring plan. Perfiliev clinched their opposition by circulating three documents supporting the claim that Boutros-Ghali intended to downgrade all UN programs that were not popular with the U.S. government. The secretary-general was subsequently forced by a majority of the UN membership in the General Assembly to alter his reform plan significantly.

The three documents were later revealed to be forgeries. Thus, Perfiliev was left somewhat exposed. So in January 1998, Perfiliev told the UN Office of Internal Oversight Services that opposition to the secretary-general's reform plan had really been "incited" by a Russian UN official whom Perfiliev had earlier targeted for bureaucratic execution. (Another charge leveled by Perfiliev against that infelicitous Russian was that of being too friendly with U.S. UN ambassador Richardson.) On the evidence of Perfiliev and his subordinates, the oversight committee found that "on the balance of probability" the targeted official must have conspired against the secretary-general and recommended that Perfiliev's hapless victim be suspended with pay pending consideration of the case by the UN joint disciplinary committee.

Perfiliev continued systematically to cleanse the Secretariat of the few Russians who previously had not submitted to the demands of the KGB with the desired alacrity. But there is reason to withhold extreme judgment on Perfiliev, for he had ample cause to fear that the few newly Americanized Russian UN staff members might make a case against him as a foreign spy working for a member state—although perhaps two-thirds of the UN Secretariat staff could be subject to those charges based on similar suspicions.

In a revealing postscript, Perfiliev gradually gained influence with Undersecretary-General Joseph Connor, the former CEO of Pricewater-house. This welcome connection gave Perfiliev ample reason to rely on the support of the U.S. government for his efforts to derail the reform program being blandly sponsored by the U.S. government.

*   *   *

The Oil-for-Food scandal is a potent indictment of the way business is done at the UN Secretariat. It represents the ongoing impeachment of the UN system, a symbol of continuing massive corruption involving the theft of close to $11 billion in revenues.

Oil-for-Food was originally set up in 1995 to compensate for the re-strictions put on Iraq after the Gulf War. The trade embargoes and sanc-tions imposed on the government of Saddam Hussein in order to prevent the pursuit of Iraqi weapons programs had also imposed osten-sible hardships on the Iraqi people. Therefore, a program was inaugu-rated under UN auspices allowing Iraq to sell unlimited quantities of oil. The proceeds were to be used to buy humanitarian supplies and to cover reparations for the victims of Iraqi aggression during the 1991 Gulf War.

In 1996, Kofi Annan, then undersecretary-general for disarmament and peacekeeping, was chosen by Secretary-General Boutros-Ghali to straighten out the program, which was not producing any tangible re-sults. Kofi relied in turn upon the help of private sector brokers. Among them was Kofi's own son Kojo, working in tandem with another privi-leged individual, Leo Mugabe, nephew of President Robert Mugabe of Zimbabwe.

Seven years later, on November 20, 2003, before the "unforgiving" glare of the UN Security Council, Benon V. Sevan—now head of this humanitarian program appointed by Kofi Annan as secretary-general—

delivered the ultimate official accounting for that program on the eve of its transfer to U.S. military authorities. Sevan did so proudly, stating that "nobody has been able to point a finger about any corruption with all the money involved."

Sevan's accounting described in general terms the magnitude of the Oil-for-Food Program, which between 1996 and 2003 had totaled $67 billion in oil exports and $31 billion in supplies of food and medicine delivered to the Iraqi people, leaving $8.2 billion in humanitarian goods still to be delivered. In addition, Sevan explained, $3 billion had gone into a development fund to rebuild Iraq.

"We did a good job under very difficult circumstances. We were caught up between different groups at different times, shifting political interests, shifting economic interests," Sevan told the Security Council in summing up his assessment of the Oil-for-Food activities, which he himself had supervised. And who better to judge the excellence and pro-bity of those who run any program, than the person who is right there running it all along!

Upon his return to New York, Sevan took some time out to rest in his newly acquired Eastern Long Island home, valued at $1.5 million, with its swimming pool and tennis court on four acres of prime residen-tial real estate, and perhaps also to relax in his second home, a new lux-ury apartment on New York's posh Upper East Side.

Accountings of the sort that Sevan presented to the Security Coun-cil have to be expressed in general terms, since they were delivered be-fore the Council, an organization that is occupied with critical security issues and thus too busy for specific details. Still, a not-unreasonable critic might wonder how $67 billion of oil exported from Iraq equated with $31 billion in food and humanitarian goods and $8.2 billion still in the pipeline. That would add up to $67 billion out versus $39.2 bil-lion back in, plus another $3 billion for development, for a total back into Iraq of $42.2 billion. The clarifying figure of $46 billion, allegedly received by the time Saddam was finally deposed by the United States, gives the layman little comfort, for we do not know how much came in from Iraqi oil sales between the time the dictator was toppled and the time in November 2003 when Sevan reported to the UN Security Council.

Certainly it was reassuring to hear Mr. Sevan express his confidence that the U.S.-led coalition would be able to manage the program as well as he had up to that point. Unfortunately, however, a short while before the turnover, Sevan announced that accurate financial records of the Oil-for-Food Program could not be found due to the bombing of UN headquarters in Baghdad. It would not be unreasonable to wonder what such important financial records were doing in Baghdad without duplicate records being kept in UN headquarters in New York in these days of digitalized computer filing.

Benon Sevan was put in charge of the Oil-for-Food Program in 1997. A well-known figure in the UN Secretariat over the previous fifteen years, Sevan has had considerable experience in UN Middle East ventures. Among other things, he is remembered for being partial to Mohammed Najibullah, who was made president of Afghanistan by the Soviet Union in 1979 and who, as head of the Afghan secret police, became notorious for his brutality and ruthlessness. Najibullah was ousted in 1992 and later sheltered in a UN compound by Benon Sevan, where in 1996 he was captured by the rebels and hanged. The subsequent takeover by the Taliban was to a significant degree a result of the ineptitude of the United Nations, which took the side of the unpopular, Soviet-backed regime of Najibullah.

Benon Sevan, along with Iqbal Riza and other veteran Secretariat colleagues, have all been known as poker-playing cronies of Kofi Annan. Kofi has rewarded them by giving them pivotal posts in the UN Secretariat in spite of their less-than-impeccable professional background.

Today Sevan forcefully denies that there has been any secrecy in the administration of the Oil-for-Food Program, which involved a French bank, BNP Paribas, not arbitrarily chosen in tandem with Cotecna, S.A. to issue letters of credit to most Oil-for-Food Program suppliers. According to Sevan, hundreds of audits were conducted in five years. What was not made public was which suppliers and which countries got how much—in other words, the hundreds of audits, property of the UN, were secret. Moreover, the Coalition Provisional Authority (CPA) took over the UN Oil-for-Food Program in November 2003 with no known audits having been conducted to ascertain the reliability of whatever figures were turned over by the UN.

During the execution of this massive program, 890 UN staff members and 3,600 Iraqis were involved—not to mention the additional participation of suppliers and Iraqi government officials who implemented the loosely defined program. Any records kept of the Oil-for-Food activities have gone through several metamorphoses and conversions. Therefore, all we have left in the public domain is the vivid recollection that Kofi Annan launched the program with the assistance of a firm brought into the Oil-for-Food Program by his son Kojo and Kojo's associate Leo Mugabe.

Sevan assures his critics that the UN Oil-for-Food Program has been one of the most efficient UN programs ever. After all, it was established to deal with a humanitarian crisis and it was run by the United Nations and has, consequently, received the UN seal of approval in retrospect. All of this might be accepted at face value as a certification of integrity.

But chronically "suspicious" organizations such as the U.S. General Accounting Office (GAO) have revealed that Saddam Hussein generated $6.6 billion in illicit earnings through surcharges and oil smuggling between 1997 and 2001. Other official estimates from the United Kingdom claim that the GAO figure is conservative and that Saddam's skimming may have amounted to more than $10 billion. The U.S. Congress has gone further, estimating the amount at $21 billion.

The UN Oil-for-Food Program oversaw a huge flow of funds from oil sales in Iraq, an amount five times greater than the entire UN budget. These funds were to be only administered by the UN, and not appropriated, diverted, or stolen for personal use by the officials running the program. The UN Oil-for-Food Program manipulated funds in trust, funds not assigned to the UN as part of its budget. Thus the UN has no excuse—even a specious one—to keep the exact, detailed figures secret. This accounting is not proprietary to the United Nations. It wasn't their money.

The UN must justify the trust placed upon its officials by a UN Security Council resolution (UNSC Res. 986), which calls on the UN Secretariat to perform an international public service. The emphasis is on public. Yet even from the meager data made available by the UN on the financial manipulations performed by the Oil-for-Food Program, it is evident that Saddam Hussein's politics played a large role in the delivery by the Oil-for-Food Program of funds intended for humanitarian purposes. Fifty percent or more of the amount earned by Iraqi oil sales under the program and allocated to Iraqi Kurdistan had not been delivered by March 2003. Nearly $4 billion of Iraqi Kurdistan Oil-for-Food funds remained in the bank—that is, unspent—for more than five years on Saddam's orders.

Under the UN's Oil-for-Food Program, Iraq's oil revenues ($67 billion) were put into an "escrow account." These funds were to be released by the UN only to pay for food and other items approved by the UN sanctions committee. Cotecna, S.A. was the UN's "independent" inspection agent. All relevant paperwork on imports was presented to Cotecna, which then certified that a consignment of goods purchased with Oil-for-Food funds had been made available for inspection, after which suppliers transported the goods to delivery locations in Iraq.

Cotecna was a Swiss firm set up to supervise and certify international business transactions, much like Lloyds of London. Cotecna used to belong to a Swiss-based multinational company, Société Générale de Surveillance. That company was involved in various scandals, among them several involving Benazir Bhutto, which were investigated by Jules Kroll Associates. Cotecna was sold back by S.G.S. to its original owners in 1997. Cotecna also employed Kofi Annan's son Kojo, and subsequently indirectly employed the Kojo Annan–Leo Mugabe consulting firm, which brought Cotecna to Iraq when Kojo's father was put in charge of the Oil-for-Food Program in 1996. Since then, Cotecna has had the UN contract for verifying compliance with the UN Oil-for-Food Program.

Kojo Annan and Leo Mugabe had set up a very successful enterprise in Zimbabwe that contracted to develop (at enormous cost overruns) the Harare International Airport as well as President Mugabe's fabulous mansions. They did business also with the corruption-ridden administration of Laurent Kabila in the Congo. The Kojo-Leo enterprise was registered in the Isle of Man as Air Harbour Technologies. Brought to Iraq by his father, Kojo in turn brought Cotecna—in spite of the firm's dubious antecedents—into the Oil-for-Food Program as insurer and main instrument for the fraudulent certification that led to a system of kickbacks and cozy deals with UN officials, such as the sale of Iraqi oil to a Panamanian-registered firm in fact controlled by Benon Sevan.

In typical UN fashion, the entire Oil-for-Food operation was being handled as proprietary UN business, safe from inquiry from the press or the U.S. government. The scheme would have succeeded without a hitch had not Saddam Hussein's regime been overthrown and the Oil-for-Food Program been transferred in all its mysterious splendor to the U.S.-led coalition in Iraq.

In a recent report to the UN Security Council, Kofi Annan asked that Cotecna, S.A. be retained by the Coalition Provisional Authority to continue to perform future authentication services. Meanwhile, Sevan declared that there were instances of inflated receipts, which "we don't investigate ourselves. If we have the documents indicating fraud we bring it [*sic*] to the notice of the relevant country and they should investigate. But there are so many brokers. You find the one you are after is dealing with another broker, and by the time you get to them they have disappeared."

Was the Oil-for-Food scandal a matter of careless oversight by Kofi Annan, who, as UN secretary-general, might be expected to administer personally a program of such unprecedented financial magnitude? The benefit of the doubt cannot be tendered, since it was through his intervention, when he was UN undersecretary-general, that he brought in his own son, and as a result the main agent in the corruption cover-up, Cotecna, S.A., was introduced into the equation. Benon Sevan, presently the cynosure of suspicious eyes for his likely direct benefit from the kickback schemes, was also brought in by Kofi as his trusted friend and protégé. Thus, the UN program that was instituted to alleviate the suffering of the Iraqi people became a travesty that enriched Saddam Hussein, provided him ample funds for procuring arms and bribing journalists and politicians all over the world, and benefited a corrupt Swiss firm that certified a shameful cover-up.

Finally, as pressures mounted from the press, respected syndicated columnists, radio and TV talk shows, and from many other pressure points that created discomfort for the UN secretary-general and his Oil-for-Food collaborators at the UN, an investigation seemed expedient, commissioned by—who else?—Kofi Annan, the prime suspect.

The Oil-for-Food scandal has hit the American public as a revelation of strange behavior at the United Nations. In fact, this very recent scandal is not an aberration at the UN. It forms part of a pattern that can be considered the norm.

CHAPTER TWELVE

The UN Jihad

I had on my UN staff mostly Russians and Middle Easterners. To the poor Russians (who usually did as they were told by their masters, or else) I could not relate for a long time on a totally relaxed basis. In the mid-1980s, however, the Middle Eastern staff members at the UN were ostensibly America's friends, and everyone trusted and liked them. My Middle Eastern guys introduced me to their compatriots throughout the Secretariat—Algerians, Moroccans, Libyans, Iraqis, Iranians, Afghans, and others. They didn't give a damn about the gold shield in my wallet.

The Delegates Lounge in the UN complex is a large, relaxing place with a bar and short-order restaurant on a mezzanine above it. The lounge is quite a tourist attraction because, besides being the upper-class social club of the UN Secretariat, it displays an enormous tapestry of the Great Wall of China woven in China, apparently following a projection from a panoramic photograph. It resembles a huge postcard. This tapestry is one of the dozen or so vulgar wonders of the world. There are lounge chairs and tables everywhere. You can go there and lounge with impunity for the whole day. Many Secretariat staff members, with nothing much to occupy their "working" hours, spend a lot of their time at the lounge. Some practically live there. Complimentary computers are provided for those wishing to surf the Web.

After months of visits at lunchtime, I began to notice that the center portion of the lounge was consistently occupied, from about 11:00 A.M. to 3:00 P.M., by a large group. Among them were members of my staff and their friends whom I had met—all Middle Eastern or North African. There were also various midlevel staff members from the Middle Eastern and North African missions to the UN.

They always spoke Arabic, and the center of attraction was the UN delegate from the PLO, their leader—or so it appeared.

Whenever I approached any of those whom I knew, the conversation, even if it was in Arabic, would stop. The reaction to my frequent greetings was always friendly enough, but I was never asked to join the group.

One day, a bit miffed at the automatic silence brought about by my proximity, I said, "You guys don't have to stop talking Arabic. I don't speak the language or any of its dialects." A group member I had not yet met replied, "But you speak Spanish, and we all know that Spanish has many words derived from Arabic."

I laughed. The remark was meant as a joke, an embellishment of the truth. "So does English," I said. "Like cotton, which comes from *al katan* in Arabic."

"So, you do know some Arabic!" he exclaimed.

I mentioned this daily phenomenon to my deputy, Carlos Casap, a Bolivian who coincidentally was of Arab ancestry. He said, "Don't you know who those fellows are? They are a loose organization representing conservative or fundamentalist Arab and other Islamic interests who meet there regularly—every day—to map out strategy and coordinate their activities. They believe that their culture and religion are threatened, inter alia, by the Russians, by the Europeans of course, by the curse of Israel, but primarily by this country—the United States."

Bibi Netanyahu knew about the Islamic cabal. What he didn't know was precisely what they were up to. Neither did I, at first. But I was able to observe that those among them who were members of my staff, and other of their compatriots working near our offices, returned to their own workstations at about 3:00 P.M., after the meetings broke up. Then they became busily engaged in strange activities—occasionally in a frenzied manner. What they did on such occasions seemed to bear no relation to the meager tasks being assigned to them in the Secretariat.

Let me review the traditional UN Secretariat work schedule. For most staff members, UN Secretariat workdays begin at around 10:00 A.M. Lunch hour really starts at noon, even though the custom is to sit down to eat somewhere around 1:30, and the midday repast is seldom over before about 3:00 P.M. By 4:30, on the pretext of beating the threatening rush-hour traffic, many staff members prepare to depart.

But as far as I could determine, the Islamic members of my office that flocked together with their buddies in the Delegates Lounge frequently worked assiduously from 3:00 P.M. until 5:30, much longer than most other people.

The UN Romanian permanent representative, Ambassador Aurel Dragos Munteanu, who arrived at the UN in 1986, chaired some committees with me and became a close friend. He had a very different view of the "Islamic conspiracy," for it was thus that he referred to the group of thirty or so who met without fail at the Delegates Lounge.

A Romanian Jew, Munteanu had been sent to the UN to get along with the Americans. The U.S. was a country the ruling Ceauşescu regime considered to be dominated by the international "Jewish" conspiracy. After all, didn't we have in our government people like Kissinger, Weinberger, Schlesinger, and Goldwater? I told Munteanu, who had a keen sense of humor, that Goldwater ran for president but lost. "Who's counting?" he jested.

One day Munteanu and I repaired to the Delegates Lounge and sat on the periphery of the UN Islamic "jihad." I began to mention to Munteanu in a normal tone of voice the plight of Israel, which had no friends in the Secretariat besides me. Aurel became very agitated and insisted that we leave the premises immediately. "Are you insane to identify me with Israel in front of that gang of cutthroats? I can't afford to appear even the slightest bit compromised. They already know I am a Jew!"

"Nobody could hear us," I countered.

"You never know who can and who can't hear us," he said. "Besides, in the Romanian mission I have three very good Securitate agents, who work in the UN Secretariat, of course. I'll tell Nicolae to talk to you frankly. My boys know what they are doing, and they tell me almost every day that those Arabs are closely related to the terrorist groups throughout the Middle East and can target anyone they want, dispensing whatever fate they choose to mete out. Pedro, you are the top American spy around here. You are not an Israeli. Keep your nose clean on the Israeli issue. Those Arab guys don't kid around!"

I assessed Munteanu as the product of a police state where indiscretions could cost anyone dearly. His paranoia would naturally carry over to an international arena, but at the UN, cutting throats and things like that were not the order of the day.

Still I had considerable respect for his top Securitate operative, Nicolae Ion, who supposedly worked for me on my staff.

I asked Ion to my office one day, pretending to have read and admired a boring, mindless tract authored by his "great" leader Ceauşescu, which Ion had presented to me earlier. After a little chat, I managed to steer the conversation to the Islamic group that met regularly in the Delegates Lounge.

"Mr. Sanjuan, they are representing all the extreme organizations in the Middle East and North Africa . . . you know . . . that fight the Jews. Here they say they love America, but they hate American Jews, and they think the American government is controlled either by Jews or, how you say, 'Jew lovers.' They are well organized and have many supporters, including the secretary-general himself, and our own Carlos Casap, who, you know, is an Arab, too, and that mysterious lawyer type, the Pakistani renegade who sold the pictures to the Iranians." He was referring to Iqbal Riza, who later became chief of staff under Kofi Annan.

Currently popular in the UN Secretariat is the notion—widely spread around not just by Muslim extremists—that the World Trade Center destruction was actually caused by agents of Israel's Mossad intent on wrecking any Palestinian peace initiative. This is still a popular view held by a significant number of Secretariat employees who exchange comments at the UN cafeteria and other places of social congregation.

The daily meetings in the lounge went on even when I was working at the Secretariat in the eighties and nineties. But I subsequently learned that a confirmed Islamic extremist cabal now meets in an even more open environment than the public Delegates Lounge. On Fridays from 1:00 P.M. to midafternoon, Islamic services are celebrated at the UN's Dag Hammarskjöld Library.

What do officially recognized and sanctioned Islamic religious services represent when held in a large, formal space at the UN Secretariat? Every Friday afternoon beginning at 1:00 P.M. and continuing for several hours, this official religious function stands out as the recognition by the UN of a very special relationship. Catholics do not have similar facilities. Out of the 6,000 or more employees in the UN Secretariat, probably as many as 500 devout Catholics would attend early mass every day at the UN if the consecrated facilities were available. Buddhists would probably benefit from some kind of convenient temple, and so forth for the many adherents of various other religions represented by members at the UN.

The Islamic mosque arrangement, even more than the conspicuous conspiratorial gathering of anti-Israeli activists in the Delegates Lounge, represents partiality or even partisanship on the part of the UN administration—its leadership—not with the Islamic faith as such, but with the present Islamic cause, a narrow-focused, fundamentalist political movement in fact.

Was there indeed a formal mosque at the UN after 9/11? I had to see for myself. I therefore decided a while ago to infiltrate the Islamic services conducted on Friday afternoons in the so-called "penthouse" above the Dag Hammarskjöld Library.

I proceeded to the UN "penthouse," took off my shoes along with other male members of the UN professional and clerical staff on the first landing of the stairs that led to the place, and climbed the rest of the way in my socks, which, to my distress, had a hole in each.

The large penthouse chamber is flanked by rows of ten-foot-tall windows on both sides. Slowly, it filled up with worshipers, about three hundred men, who assumed the various positions of devotion required in the Islamic service.

As I sat on the floor, I realized that, in the midst of this large congregation, I could not discreetly take any photographs, even with a small digital camera. So I excused myself, alleging a painful back problem, and went to the back to stand against the rear wall. There I would be able to photograph the proceedings with much less risk of being challenged.

As I shot my pictures, I tried to appear innocuous, with the camera hidden between the palms of my hands. I looked around with a benign smile, pretending to have only a kind of nonchalant interest in the proceedings.

Furtively, five or six female worshipers entered from the rear, veiled and humble, and huddled against the back wall. They were there, these few UN women staffers, as inferior appendages to the battalion-strength male congregation. The women looked at me with a mixture of curiosity and apprehension. I guess that, as a man, I was incongruously placing myself in a position of female humiliation by leaning against the back wall.

Why does the UN Secretariat, an avowedly secular organization, currently sponsor such Islamic religious gatherings on a scheduled basis? In contrast, the Dalai Lama, a recipient of the Nobel Peace Prize, continues to be banned from all premises at the UN because the Chinese government will not tolerate a Buddhist leader on the grounds of an international organization.

And what about the secretary-general? Should I not have brought this militant Islamic conspiracy to his attention while I was still a member of the UN staff? Well, I did do exactly that—twelve years ago. These conspirators were then regarded as primarily oriented toward destroying the state of Israel, a member state of the United Nations. It must be pointed out again that the use of the UN as a gathering place for Islamic fundamentalists has been a continuing phenomenon in evidence since 1983, when I first arrived at the UN Secretariat. It has only grown more blatant with the passage of time.

To begin with, Javier Pérez de Cuellar disliked Jews the way many Latin American pseudo-aristocrats dislike Jews—not more than is required by the rules of proper social behavior. "Why does your friend Jeane Kirkpatrick keep that loud and impolite Charles Lichenstein in her office? He is a rabid Jewish militant and does not believe in the best interests of the United States here at the UN." The secretary-general asked me this after Chuck, sitting in for Jeane in the Security Council, had suggested to the Soviet representatives that if they didn't like New York, they could pack up and go back to Russia, and that he, Chuck, would be at the dock waving them good-bye. "You know, Sanjuan, Lichenstein forgets that you bid good-bye to the Russians at an airport these days," Javier pointed out with a self-satisfied smile.

When I finally broached with him the issue of the jihadist meetings conducted every day in the Delegates Lounge, he retorted, "But that is a private social club, so to speak. Anyone has a right to meet there and talk about any subject. Even Nazis can meet there, for all I care." The secretary-general's sympathy was obviously not too great as I pushed forth complaints about the militant Islamic, anti-Semitic, and anti-U.S. activities that were being carried on so blatantly in the Delegates Lounge.

Yet it would be only fair to ask what any secretary-general could have done about such complaints, even had he wanted to.

Fancy, if you will, a well-documented complaint being presented to any secretary-general. "Well-documented" implies verifiable information gathered by UN security investigations, the results of which would be made available to the secretary-general.

First of all, the UN secretary-general has no security investigators worthy of the name. The security people at the UN have no power to poke their noses into anybody's business unless it involves an overt criminal act such as armed robbery in the halls or restrooms, murder on the fire escape, throwing heavy objects such as computer monitors out of upper-story windows, or entering reserved parking areas without a properly issued (or counterfeited) parking permit.

UN security people also investigate staff suicides (jumping out of windows), of which there have been a few. In December 2003 a UN guard blew his brains out in the Indonesian Lounge.

Still, let us say that a hypothetical secretary-general did want to do something to prevent clandestine and well-organized Islamic militant operations from being conducted at the UN.

The moment such a secretary-general raised a question about one, several, or many staff members taking part in illicit political extremist activities in the headquarters, the ambassador of the country each staff member represented would lodge a strongly worded protest about the unfairness and discrimination and politically motivated persecution (undoubtedly of American origin) being heaped upon his virtuous compatriots. Multiply that protest by fifteen or twenty similar complaints if the entire militant conspiracy feared being disbanded. The reader may well understand that secretaries-general are in no position to survive such a counterblast—especially since the ones who are not hypothetical are not selected for their courageous qualities, but rather for their weakness and certified reputations as ineffectuals.

Indeed, security in general is conducted in a totally perfunctory manner at the UN. Security is not fashionable—not the UN type of thing to do. Why? In part because the absurd conceit at the UN has been all along that the organization is impelled by such a benevolent and noble purpose, everywhere recognized as such, that nobody on the outside would want to do it any harm. The general feeling is still something on the order of "We're exempt!"

You do not even have to travel beyond the perimeter of midtown Manhattan to see for yourself how incompetent security precautions are at the UN.

Recently an unsightly wall was built around the place. But wear a business suit—man or woman—and go to the Forty-eighth Street and First Avenue visitors' entrance of the United Nations. You will be directed as a visitor to a cumbersome series of temporary structures, which you will not enter. Instead, meander around for a little while and go around these structures, behind which are some steps. Descend the steps, turn right, and you will be facing a set of doors in front of the rose garden. Hang around or pretend to be smoking a cigarette.

The double doors there will be opened frequently by staffers coming out for a cigarette or a walk around the rosebushes. (The doors open only from the inside.) You may then hold one of the doors open and enter the UN premises, pretending to be a UN staff member going back into the building. As a matter of fact, a small group of UN staffers may already be there who will go in with you.

Now you are in the building, free to go wherever you wish. If you want to reach a special destination and do not know the way, ask anybody, even a UN guard—they wear light blue uniforms and are very polite.

Of course, if this clever method is too clandestine for your timid taste, then enter the aforementioned temporary structures and pretend to be a tourist. You will be admitted in that capacity and, after paying a modest fee, will go into the building with a gawking group and a guide. At any point during the tour you can easily walk away. You will be in the building.

You may also gain access to the building, initially as a tourist, by turning right after you pass by the metal detectors for tourists, taking an elevator to the basement, and going into the UN Secretariat through the parking garage.

Do not stare at the drug transactions that may be going down in the garage, for this indeed could be dangerous.

Of course, with a little more effort and sophistication, you can get some Libyan diplomat friend to lend you a parking permit such as UN diplomats put on the windshields of their cars. You can have it copied and laminated around New York's Times Square for about ten dollars. Return the original to its rightful owner. Then you can bring your own car into the garage.

One might think that reading these instructions could bring to the attention of the higher levels of the UN Secretariat the pathetic careless-ness with which they handle security. But, frankly, I doubt it.

The September 11 killers were amazingly successful. Not only did they commit unpredictable carnage, but they devastated New York's business center (eight huge buildings), temporarily paralyzed the stock market and airlines, seriously destabilized the American economy and along with it the world economy, and, supposedly, changed our entire way of life.

Pure luck? Chance? Coincidence?

A recent UN report on terrorism concluded that the 9/11 conspira-tors worked alone and managed to attack the U.S. on a very limited budget. Such conclusions are highly suspicious and suggest either a cover-up for terrorist activities the UN does not want to examine in depth or an example of the superficiality and incompetence of UN inves-tigations. Why should the UN be in a position to determine the nature of the actions of a group of individuals scattered across the United States, when the FBI and the Homeland Security people have not come to any definite conclusions on 9/11 yet?

To succeed in such a well-coordinated manner, the World Trade Center attackers had to be able to process a large amount of informa-tion—a skill and access not available to nineteen or more would-be ter-rorist martyrs skulking around hotels, motels, and airports and getting training in fly-by-night schools of aviation. The information they needed had to be gathered, processed, refined, and made available in a usable context by others who had diverse capabilities at their disposal. The UN estimate of a modest two-hundred-thousand-dollar investment in the operation that brought America to its knees is a ludicrous miscalculation that, under an earlier Cold War scenario, would have been rejected as "disinformation."

To acquire all of this refined data and select this target, coconspira-tors had to gain access to building specifications and plans obtainable from the NYC Department of Buildings by paying a fee and showing the proper credentials. To understand the significance of the data, peo-ple with more than just a superficial knowledge of engineering had to evaluate the World Trade Center's vulnerabilities, which were not really obvious to the naked eye. The aircraft struck at the most vulnerable level of both buildings at an angle calculated to inflict maximum damage and cause both to collapse from the upper stories downward. These precise vulnerabilities were studied extensively prior to the approval in New York of the WTC construction plans and have been available to qualified applicants.

Just prior to the 2004 presidential election, Osama bin Laden said in a tape that attacking the Trade Center towers was an original idea that just came to him. Such a tooth fairy claim provokes laughter. To acquire and evaluate this information and produce a coordinated plan for the destruction of the WTC, the Pentagon, and possibly the White House itself, resources were needed way in excess of two hundred thousand dollars.

What was needed and evidently available to those who executed this horror was a central intelligence-gathering facility that was immune from outside interference: a center located in New York—not isolated in Florida or Munich or Cairo, and certainly not in a rugged cave high among the impregnable crags of the Hindu Kush.

The same has to be said about the attackers of government installations in Washington, D.C. To piece together a working plan to hit the Pentagon from the air with impunity and on the executive side of the building must have taken better intelligence resources than those at the disposal of nineteen or so committed martyrs roaming around the country without security clearance access to the Pentagon. Such intelligence can be procured only by patient analysts working at an intelligence-gathering facility in the United States itself. An intelligence operation must have supported the attack, and that network still remains intact.

At present the Department of Homeland Security must exclude from any ongoing investigation the protected territory of the UN Secretariat in New York. Even after creating the secretary of homeland security's efficient, unified command comprising the Customs Service, the Border Patrol, the Coast Guard, a federal airport security service, and guidance from other federal law enforcement agencies, none of them can enter the UN. The 9/11 Commission was also incapable of probing into the role of some Islamic fundamentalist and jihadist groups in the UN Secretariat. I discussed the issue at length with one of the commissioners, who admitted the futility of even attempting to penetrate the immunity caparison of the UN.

Maintaining an out-of-date cloak of secrecy over the goings-on at the UN Secretariat endangers the safety of the people in New York and any other city that may be a target of terrorism.

This is not a call for a general war between Islam and the West at the UN. But there is an atmosphere—an ethos, if you will—of extreme Islamic fervor within the halls of the UN, an organization originally created to prevent war that is expected to remain secular and nonpolitical.

Muslim extremists consider secular states infidel territory. They are in their own way internationalists in that they are apparently continuing, with varying degrees of success, to convert the Secretariat and other UN agencies into an international staging area that supports militant Islamic causes. For a long time these militant Islamic groups have been assisted by nothing more sinister than the tolerance of UN secretaries-general to Muslim religious and political activities inside the Secretariat. That includes Kofi Annan, the present secretary-general, although his predecessors were, in a sense, much more complicitous. Kofi Annan's predecessors deliberately coddled Muslim extremism on a daily basis through their undisguised anti-Semitism in an atmosphere that equated Zionism not only with racism but with the United States as a whole.

Mohammed Atta, once one of the suspected leaders of the WTC plot, set up an Islamic prayer group using the facilities at the Technical University of Hamburg-Harburg, which German police believe provided cover for Islamic militant and terrorist planning activities. The militants were there for a long time but betrayed no noticeable connections with terrorist or criminal acts—yet it is suspected with good reason that this and other Islamic centers played a role in assisting Mr. Atta or his colleagues in their plan to destroy a large part of New York City.

Intelligence authorities were quoted by the *New York Times* on September 23, 2003, as having tracked a network of terrorist-affiliated business dealings that encompassed banking, export-import firms, agricultural companies, and other outfits all over the world. This is described as an empire that moves people and money around. The Islamic extremist network operates in sixty countries and, according to U.S. intelligence officials, no one knows how far the Taliban's reach has really extended. A NATO ambassador in Brussels has been quoted as saying, "The international system is so globalized, so instant, with so many opportunities and anonymity that these guys can take advantage of it."

The second Bush administration contacted police departments throughout the world to create a global antiterrorist network, more than three thousand people in thirty countries. But Interpol's budget of about $25 million probably pales in contrast to bin Laden's intelligence budget and to the funds and facilities that are available to run an efficient central nexus. In addition we have to take into account the so-far unchallenged resources at the disposal of Islamic extremists clustered inside the UN Secretariat itself who benefit from accessible facilities and finances already in place and, at present, total immunity.

The FBI can observe and follow foreign UN mission diplomats anywhere around the City of New York—to hotels, movies, supermarkets, schools, public parks, or anywhere they choose to wander in New York—except for one big place in mid-Manhattan. That place, of course, is the United Nations headquarters compound.

For years, Iraqi and Afghan diplomats associated with the Taliban have spent a good deal of their working day in that UN compound—frequently meeting with their comrades and compatriots. Their compeers all have offices in the UN Secretariat and are amply provided with ostensibly secure telephones, computers, and access to their own UN Secretariat bank, a Chase Manhattan branch made available for use by UN Secretariat staffers and staffed from Chase's large pool of competent foreign employees.

Why have these Iraqi and Taliban diplomats met in the past for extended periods in the UN Secretariat along with Mr. Nasser al-Kidwa, the PLO representative at the United Nations, nephew of Yasser Arafat? As we have already shown, they have all met for years in the UN Delegates Lounge, along with UN Secretariat staff members who have expressed known Islamic militant views.

The question therefore obviously arises as to why, in today's environment, our country's law enforcement investigators may not examine these extremists' activities. What are the Taliban sympathizers and Saddam Hussein's former agents as well as agents of Hezbollah, Islamic Jihad, Hamas, and similar groups up to inside the UN Secretariat? Why follow these people around New York within a radius of twenty-five miles from Columbus Circle, when their most dangerous operations must of necessity be those they perform inside the UN building?

Certainly the UN building is a perfect environment for Islamic militant activities that for a long time have been carried out within a clandestine, organized grouping that endures even as UN secretaries-general come and go. The UN provides a friendly atmosphere for these elements in a place where blatant anti-Semitism holds sway. It is a friendly atmosphere where, upon the spread of news about the World Trade Center disaster, clusters of anti-American sympathizers on the staff openly expressed their glee that at last America was getting what it deserved, not very different from the celebrations by Palestinians captured on TV immediately after 9/11.

A well-meaning person may say, "Well, they could be watched and prevented from engaging in illegal or criminal activities by UN authorities inside the UN Secretariat."

But this is hardly likely, is it? This cannot be done inside an organization that has permitted and now still condones:

* the sale of shotguns by members of its disarmament department as well as the sale of controlled substances used in the manufacture of nuclear weapons;
* the most flagrant forms of nepotism and favoritism and cronyism;
* the diversion of millions of dollars in UN funds to a huge accounting firm;
* the flagrant operation of a vast foreign intelligence collection

activity directed at obtaining information to undermine the
defense capabilities of the host country—the United States;

- the exclusion of a competent and loyal American official for
  not brazenly lying to the U.S. Congress;
- the infiltration and glorification of heads of large organized
  crime syndicates;
- the total corruption of entire sectors of its overseas
  operations, such as the scandalous criminal activities
  conducted by UN officials throughout all of East Africa,
  and the Oil-for-Food Program in Iraq;
- the customary requirement by UN officials of taking bribes
  from companies that want to do business with the UN, paid
  by movers, travel agencies, and computer software
  companies.

The notion of monitoring the activities of different illegal, criminal,
corrupt, and terrorist-oriented groups or individuals operating under
the cover of UN immunity might still have seemed unacceptable to
many people before the events of September 11, 2001. Their argument
would have been that such illegal UN activities—those that have done
so much damage to the people of East Africa—are a price society has to
pay, particularly when hosting an international organization. The injury
these corrupt and criminal elements perpetrate within the UN may affect the welfare of the American people as well as people in other parts
of the world, but that comes with the territory, the permissive UN supporters would say.

After September 11, 2001, that permissive perspective surely must
change, not because of blind fear, but because of the need to take intelligent countermeasures that go beyond imposing colorful alerts. It
should be quite obvious—because there is ample evidence of it—that
the UN Secretariat, immune from outside oversight, fiscally irresponsi-
ble, and very accessible to terrorists, is an obvious shelter we cannot afford to ignore.

CHAPTER THIRTEEN

The Travesty of "Reform"

Whatever creates a better system to preserve political and economic stability at the UN should obviously be encouraged. So it was gratifying when Secretary-General Kofi Annan publicly welcomed the adoption in 2003 by the UN General Assembly of an anticorruption convention. "Corruption is a key element in economic under-performance and a major obstacle to poverty alleviation and development," Kofi announced. Amen! "Corrupt officials will, in future, find fewer ways to hide their illicit gains," he added.

Three days later, on November 3, 2003, the former head of Mexico's anticrime unit resigned from the UN, a man with an international reputation for fighting the toughest organized criminals in Mexico. Samuel González-Ruiz had been hired to advise the UN office on drugs and crime. In his final statement, he said, "I do not have the stomach to be promoting a fight against organized crime and corruption around the world when I am working in an organization that tolerates administrative and in some cases criminal violations." He cast particular aspersions on the UN agency in Vienna that is supposed to be fighting the narcotics trade and organized corruption.

The UN Office on Drugs and Crime (UNODC) in Vienna is made up largely of former chiefs of police from different countries. The somewhat innocent notion behind this concept is that former police chiefs are totally honest and thus best qualified to stamp out international organized crime.

González-Ruiz was one of the few former chiefs of police who had a qualifying record of accomplishment. During his service in Mexico City he was acknowledged to be extremely capable and courageous in fighting the pervasive Mexican drug cartels, with unprecedented results. When he entered the UN Office of Drugs and Crime in Vienna, he expected to be working in an atmosphere governed by at least some minimal degree of ethics and morality.

To González-Ruiz's surprise, however, the office was run by people who took advantage of a flexible budget to travel to their countries of origin at will, or through them, on the pretext of performing missions to places the travel routes to which could be craftily deflected. González-Ruiz found that patent conflicts of interest were tolerated in UNODC, such as the hiring of wives of supervisors to work under the direction of their husbands. He also found that frequent threats of retaliation against potential whistle-blowers were being made by those nominally in charge of fighting crime.

González-Ruiz and a colleague complained repeatedly, and finally he resigned in protest. He did so quite noisily. The details of his resignation were covered by the international press.

At that point an investigation was authorized by the UN secretary-general. The investigation was an in-house affair conducted by the fox who watched the chicken coop—that is, by the UN Office of Internal Oversight Services headquartered in New York. The result of this investigation produced a record that inadvertently revealed that sweet blend of malfeasance and ineptitude that we have been attempting to illustrate.

Immediately after the issuance of the report on the investigation by the UN Office of Internal Oversight Services (OIOS), the Vienna UNODC put out a press release announcing that the investigation had cleared them of all accusations. That release, issued on November 26, 2003, was ingeniously described as being "for information only—not an official document." This was to cover the gluteus maximus of the UN-

ODC in case anyone should point out that the OIOS report said nothing of the kind.

But in truth, it would have been hard to say what the report had concluded, for the alphabet soup of claims, counterclaims, delinquencies, miscues, charges, lapses of surveillance, and frequent and detailed references to the rules and regulations that the "oversighters" allege in their report either apply or do not apply to the alleged misconduct, resulted in their reaching no conclusion at all. That is precisely the purpose of a UN oversight investigation. This one was hailed as an independent process of surveillance, when it was in fact an in-house investigation and anything but independent.

The rules that applied in the case were clear to the "oversighters" and were stated in the report.

No father, mother, son, daughter, brother, or sister of a UN official shall be appointed where another person is available to fill a position.

No preference shall be given to an appointee by virtue of relationship to a staff member.

Any relative shall disqualify him or herself from any decision affecting the staff member to whom he or she is related.

The secretary-general may impose disciplinary measures on staff members whose conduct is unsatisfactory.

No staff member shall disclose to any government outside the UN any information about an investigation except by the secretary-general's authorization. These obligations do not cease upon separation from service.

These rules seem clear enough. Yet the failure to implement them was not mentioned in the investigators' report. The OIOS report seemed to say, "These are the rules that apply; this is what happened; but we are making no connection between the two. That is not our job."

In the process of investigating travel irregularities, the "oversighters" unwittingly disclosed that the Vienna drugs and crime staff did nothing but travel. Australians went to Australia; Brits went everywhere via London. But there was nothing wrong about that because it fell within UN travel guidelines. Suspicious, yes; wrong, no, the "over-sighters" said. Meanwhile, cryptic comments abound in the investigators' report, such as, "It is beyond the purview of this report to inquire into the vagaries of airline fares."

On the other hand, the report refers to the complainants somewhat darkly as perhaps having "wittingly or unwittingly" ignored certain facts. Thus the oversighters intimate that the complainants themselves may be scoundrels. That's what you get when you complain. The report also takes great pains to point out that what may appear to be a conflict in the simplistic outside world is not necessarily a conflict within the more sophisticated UN environment. For example, what is considered a bribe "in many national jurisdictions" is not always a bribe inside the UN. Therefore, the appearance of conflict of interest, which is grounds for termination in most Western (and Eastern) organizations, is not cause for alarm at the UN. Another "finding" in the OIOS investigators' report was that a partial conflict of interest—like the boss not being the only supervisor of the work done by the boss's wife—nullifies any hint of impropriety. The oversight people did acknowledge that there might have been lapses in the conduct of supervisors in the UN drug and crime office, but lapses, while unfortunate, are not technically violations, they added.

With reference to the threatened termination of the two complainants—one of whom, as we stated, soon resigned in protest—the "oversighters" concluded that since both had fixed-term appointments, the issue of retaliation was moot. That was sheer nonsense, of course. All UN appointments are fixed-term, and most are routinely renewed. Therefore, the issue of retaliation was by no means moot. The oversighters further state that since one of the complainants' positions was subsequently "restricted by excluding funds from the project," the evidence again did not support the allegation of retaliation. In fact, the very opposite was supported by the selective evidence that the OIOS indiscreetly presented in its lengthy, repetitive, and badly written report.

Toward the end of this typical UN inquiry, the investigators explain in rather amusing fashion that the complainants should not be mistaken for "whistle-blowers." "The term whistle-blower confers a legal status that provides specific protections due to a specific well-founded threat of harm; however, it is often used instead of the correct term of complainant."

In conclusion, the oversight office stated:

"Allegations when made must be carefully examined and the conduct they describe must be analyzed against legal norms and not simply characterized as wrongful or corrupt behavior. To say that someone is corrupt is harmful without purpose unless there is evidence of behavior which can be characterized under a norm."

The report further concludes:

"The Chief's past history and pattern of contracts given to his wife merits strong management response. However, the Chief's conflict of interest and poor judgment should not be used as evidence that corruption, abuse, nepotism and mismanagement are rampant in UNODC as alleged by the complainants."

Finally, the garbled Oversight Services (OIOS) report states that it was right to investigate the charges alleged. That there was a cover-up at the drug and crime office. That the staff should be knowledgeable about rules and regulations, and that "sensitization" exercises are in order and perhaps even necessary. They also conclude, however, that the complainants had talked out of school by disseminating their complaints to "donor governments" against UN rules, thereby tarnishing the image of the UN. Sanctions (punishment) against the two complainants would be recommended if they were to remain in the employ of the UN, which they were not.

To punish all the others who might be involved in anything improper, the oversighters recommended that a message be issued to the drug and crime staff in Vienna "to remind them that complaints in good faith are encouraged to be made through proper channels." The oversighters also recommend that the heads of the Vienna UN office prepare and present a course of instruction for the drug and crime managers. Finally, regarding the conflict of interest of the chief of the operations branch of the drug and crime office, "Appropriate action should be instituted." Surely a harsher punishment was never endured!

This OIOS investigation has been described here in some detail because it is typical of internal malfeasance inquiries made at the UN. The techniques of double-talk and deliberate obfuscation are used to protect the status quo and whitewash the accused.

Reform is a much abused and strangely popular term at the United Nations. For the last twenty years at least, within the span of my UN experience, the U.S. Congress has "intransigently" demanded reform, and UN secretaries-general—Javier Pérez de Cuellar, Boutros Boutros-Ghali, and Kofi Annan—have all promised reform.

Javier handled the concept of reform quite successfully. He promised reform but did not tax his intellectual resources to do anything about it. He felt that restructuring or modifying the Secretariat were matters that at most should have his blessing. That was, if nothing else, at least a moral posture.

Boutros Boutros-Ghali was the opposite, but strangely enough, the result was the same. Boutros set out to reorganize everything by means of successive waves of orders and administrative edicts. He reshuffled functions, reassigned officials, rearranged operations—but those were all symbolic gestures that left the nature and volume of UN activities undisturbed.

"Selfish" UN staff members were annoyed at the inconvenience of having to repeatedly rearrange furniture, move from one floor to the other, and amend their titles for the UN directory during Boutros's reign. At one point (in 1995) they placed signs in the UN garage that clamored—tongue in cheek—for a new reorganization, since for two months they had been left undisturbed to "fester" in one location.

None of these patent simulacrums gained Boutros much acceptance with U.S. Ambassador Madeleine Albright, who later became secretary of state. But it has to be recognized that her initial alienation had little to do with Boutros's success or failure at bringing about UN reform.

At first, Boutros appeared quite attentive to her policy suggestions and soon managed to gain her confidence. She in turn relied on him for advice, particularly in areas of the world that Boutros—who had been at one time Egypt's foreign minister—purportedly knew well.

During the Somalia crisis of 1993, Boutros advised Madeleine Albright to declare the Somali warlord Mohammed Aidid an outlaw, and she was able to enlist the U.S. government to brand him as the "outlaw" he was. A few years before, during the Egyptian-Sudanese crisis, Boutros, a Christian Copt in charge of Egypt's foreign affairs, had tangled with Aidid and considered the Somali warlord a mortal enemy. This fact may not have been known by Dr. Albright when Boutros succeeded in getting her to make his personal vendetta congruent with U.S. policy.

The U.S. adventure in Somalia to capture Aidid ended badly. American soldiers were slaughtered in Mogadishu, and the Clinton administration rapidly withdrew U.S. forces. The episode threatened to mar Dr. Albright's career plans, and she abruptly terminated her chummy relations with the UN secretary-general. Boutros, not accustomed in his native land—in spite of his French cultural pretensions—to allow a woman to humiliate him, angrily referred to her as *une femme vulgaire,* an expression that considerably transcends the meaning of "vulgar woman." Madeleine reportedly swore that she would show Boutros just how vulgar she could be and made it a personal cause to have the United States reject the reappointment of Boutros, in fact vetoing his second five-year term and personally selecting Kofi Annan to succeed him. Kofi is a sub-Saharan African with Swedish citizenship, thus eligible to be nominated as secretary-general, for the UN custom has been that no candidate will be considered who comes from a major world power or developed country. Sweden and Ghana are both considered neutrals— Ghana because it stays out of world affairs, Sweden because it attempts to meddle in everybody else's.

Thus, everything that poor Boutros had tried to do to show the U.S. Congress, the White House, the American press, and anyone else who would listen that he was a reform-minded, manic reorganizer of the UN Secretariat turned out to be wasted effort. Not only did his shuffles and reshuffles fail to achieve any beneficial result, they did not achieve even the primary objective of guaranteeing his tenure for two terms like all the other secretaries-general before him.

Kofi Annan has been far more successful than Boutros-Ghali in projecting the image of a reform-oriented secretary-general, deploring waste, inefficiency, and corruption, and advocating big structural changes in the UN Security Council. He has spoken out in favor of increasing that council's membership, from the present five permanent members—the U.S., Russia, China, the UK, and France—to up to nine or eleven, including India, Japan, Germany, and Brazil. Certainly that change would do something to make the UN more representative of the world's most populous nations, albeit not of the world's largest ethnic groups.

But it would not do much. Half of the world represented at the UN would still be dominated by the hands-on power of the other half. It is, moreover, doubtful that in either of the so-called "legislative bodies" of the UN—the Security Council and the General Assembly—structural reforms will be brought about by pressure from any secretary-general with his own personal prejudices to satisfy.

Kofi Annan should be moderately praised for paying such lip service to the need for UN parliamentary reform. But long-range, hypothetical changes in the UN Security Council or General Assembly should not be a reason to neglect other reforms that he can institute much more rapidly and without effective opposition from any of the member states. It may take some courage to fix the rotted political plumbing in the UN Secretariat, but a "reform-minded" secretary-general has to have backbone and a certain degree of integrity.

The United States is the principal bankroller of the UN as well as its principal host. Why, then, has the U.S. government not attempted to prevent widespread UN espionage operations or clandestine operations supporting terrorism against Israel and quite possibly against the United States? And why has the U.S. not protested at all effectively against the massive corruption, blatant conflicts of interest, and widespread criminal activities that thrive in the UN Secretariat?

The answer is all too simple to be easily believed by people on the outside.

The United States government has been, in fact, a contributor to the conflict of interest and corruption in the Secretariat, and frequently a witting collaborator in such illegal activities.

With regard to tolerating the outrageous anti-Semitic ethos of the UN Secretariat, the United States government (read: the Department of State) has been thoroughly complicit, particularly in view of the insistence with which this outrageous practice has been brought to their attention. All that the U.S. has been willing to do is note these conditions and, of course, deplore them—quietly.

A skeptic might point out that during the so-called "financial crisis" of the UN in 1996, when the U.S. government seemed serious about drastically reducing its contribution to the UN, both the executive branch and Congress made loud noises about the need for reform in the Secretariat and other UN agencies. But these calls for reform focused on ill-defined generalities like the bloated UN staff or the inflated UN budget. Also, considering the falling out between Madeleine Albright and Boutros Boutros-Ghali, the U.S. demands had more to do with denying Boutros his second term than with bringing about any lasting reforms. In any case, as soon as Kofi Annan was enthroned as secretary-general, the clamor for reform noticeably dissipated.

But conflict of interest has never been an issue within the UN Secretariat, as the outrageous Soviet secondment arrangement has already demonstrated. From secretaries-general on down to the lowest-level appointees, legions of staff members have been working in the UN Secretariat—supposedly an impartial international organization—in order to promote and secure the interests of their sponsoring member states. That type of conflict has always been taken for granted and expected at the UN.

In spite of this whimsical environment of unblushing conflict of interest, illegal foreign intelligence activities, traffic with organized criminals, and safe haven for Islamic extremists and terrorist sympathizers—in spite of this blatant carnival of the absurd—have no individual voices in the U.S. government been raised to challenge such abuses and travesties?

Indeed they have.

The U.S. government has been fortunate in having one whistle-

blower in particular—already alluded to—not some clerk furtively reading obscure documents in a windowless room, but a relatively high-level
official who has been blowing a loud horn to make public some of the
egregious excesses in the UN Secretariat. Here is what happened to her.

Linda Shenwick was a lawyer by training and a good bureaucrat by
profession. After rising through the ranks on merit in the U.S. government, she became an expert on UN budget and administrative practices
and, with the diplomatic rank of minister counselor, represented the
United States with distinction on something the UN calls the Advisory
Committee on Administrative and Budgetary Questions, the ACABQ.

That such a committee—theoretically supervising the use of funds at
the UN—should be advisory in nature and should deal, as its name implies, only with certain "questions" is in part due to the fact that English is
always used at the UN as a second language. The meaning of words in any
bureaucratic language is always imprecise, which makes working at the
UN sometimes a rather pleasant experience since no one has to fear any
confrontations with the cold logic of semantics—the meaning of words.

This committee is almost always referred to merely as the ACABQ,
so that its vague purview can become even more remote or diffuse. It is
the vehicle through which some member states can respectfully ask the
UN Secretariat questions about how the money they contribute to the
UN is being spent. The UN Secretariat grudgingly obliges by providing
"experts" on what is going on at the UN. These "experts" describe in
glowing terms the great success of all UN operations.

Can a member state—the United States, for example—ask to see
the UN's books, if any books are kept at all? The answer is a very diplo-
matically worded no. Many experts in the conduct of international affairs will claim that international organizations cannot function under
the direct oversight of individual member states. To open UN operations to such scrutiny would violate principles that have been evolving
since construction was begun on the Tower of Babel, the first international organization on record.

Linda Shenwick represented the United States on the ACABQ for
almost ten years. She received glowing commendations from several

American UN ambassadors appointed by both Republican and Democratic administrations. She managed, in a professional but persuasive manner, to overcome many of the obstacles the UN Secretariat put in the path of numerous budgetary investigations that concerned many types of abuses: nepotism, thievery in East Africa, outrageous expenses for the publication of frivolous and self-serving propaganda documents ($750 per page, which is more than a dismembered Gutenberg Bible would bring), and other matters that reflected criminal and dangerous activities going on inside the Secretariat and its agencies. She took her job very seriously. The only character flaw that could be ascribed to her was that perhaps she had no sense of humor. Humor is an essential qualification for survival at the UN.

Shenwick testified before Congress under oath about the thievery and other immoral excesses at the UN—$3.9 million in cash stolen in Somalia, senior UN officials hiring their wives at salaries of $70,000 or more, unnecessary and absurd plans for Secretariat departments to acquire thousands of square feet of added office space at inflated rentals in an otherwise depressed New York real estate market, and numerous other matters of that ilk.

Shenwick's reward for not perjuring herself before a congressional committee and doing her job properly at the UN was to be summarily removed from her position at the ACABQ by none other than U.S. UN ambassador Madeleine Albright. Shenwick's American successor managed to botch the next periodic election of member states to the ACABQ, and as a result the United States—the overwhelmingly largest contributor to the UN budget—was kicked out of the budget oversight committee, if with such a definition we may grace that weak institution.

Did that scandal—the in-your-face removal of the U.S. from representation in the only committee that remotely resembled an investigative fiscal branch of the UN—disturb Dr. Albright, who has never attained career status in the U.S. Senior Executive Service?

Apparently not.

The victimized American official was now graded on a periodic performance report as being derelict in her duties, which presumably required lying before Congress. She was removed from her office and placed in a windowless hole with orders not to speak unless spoken to. In other words, she was placed in what was the Department of State's very reasonable facsimile of a solitary cell at Rikers Island.

Then she was fired.

Pressure from sympathetic congressmen and senators, from liberals like Hillary Clinton and conservatives like Tom DeLay, made the Department of State transfer $5 million to another government department to create a bogus perch for our American official, perhaps a compensation for her bad treatment, but no remedy for the errors tolerated constantly by the UN budget committee. The victim refused and for a while paid a heavy price. But she serves as a warning or caution to anyone else who might get the crazy idea that taking on the abundant corruption and criminality at the UN can serve any useful purpose.

The crooks, the hardened criminals, the spies, the terrorist sympathizers, the nepotists, and the racists at the UN don't like to be interfered with. To try to call their bluff is to commit suicide without the recognition of martyrdom.

"Yo no soy de esta casa," Javier Pérez de Cuellar repeated frequently to me and to others, signifying that he was not responsible for the corrupt practices that took place at the UN under his watch, practices that people like Linda Shenwick and Conrad Stergas subsequently so courageously denounced. "I am not a part of this organization" is the actual translation of his cryptic and preposterous statement, since the title Javier bore, UN secretary-general, clearly proclaimed the opposite.

His denial seemed even more disingenuous when it became known that he had a cozy relationship with the Bank of Credit and Commerce International (BCCI), seized by British authorities after one of the most scandalous banking failures in history, involving fraud, drug profit laundering, and other illegal transactions, including financing Panamanian strongman Manuel Noriega and illegally owning banks in the United States. The BCCI, controlled by Arab financial interests, placed a Boeing 727 at the disposal of Javier Pérez de Cuellar, who used it as his personal aircraft. The plane was registered to Gaith Pharaon, an Abu Dhabi multimillionaire and a major BCCI stockholder, in apparent exchange for the secretary-general's support for Arab issues in the UN Secretariat from 1987 to 1991, when the scandal finally became public.

Similar inappropriate partisanship by Javier Pérez de Cuellar became obvious to the British and the U.S. during the battle for the Falkland Islands in 1982. In spite of the fact that the UN Security Council had condemned the Argentine invasion, Javier Pérez de Cuellar insisted on being informed by U.S. intelligence on the progress of the war and about specific intelligence information, such as where the United States was planning to refuel British bombers en route to the Falklands from the UK. These bizarre inquiries led the U.S. and the UK to keep Don Javier totally incommunicado, which he protested repeatedly.

Subsequently, Javier set up a pathetic intelligence collection operation in the UN Secretariat entitled Political Intelligence News Service. It consisted of a group of intelligence-gatherers headed by a well-known Soviet KGB agent on the staff of Undersecretary-General Ustinov to gather items of particular intelligence importance. These were to be made available on a daily basis to the secretary-general and his top staff.

The product of these labors not only failed miserably to provide information not easily found in the international press, but it became a cause célèbre featured in several hearings in the U.S. Senate by Senator Kasten. Obviously the United Nations Secretariat, a traditionally secretive operation, had no business gathering intelligence—dealing with the activities, military or otherwise, of its member states—that was not sanctioned by the UN Security Council or by the UN General Assembly.

In a sense, "I do not belong to this organization" was a statement made by Javier to reflect the fact that he did not think the UN could put any restraints on his own personal and political agenda.

*   *   *

Certainly something effective can be done to prevent the UN Secretariat from continuing as a center of political conspiracy and international intrigue. The Secretariat, even under the now totally outdated principles promoted by the victors of World War II in San Francisco, was never intended to become a foreign intelligence collection agency within the United States; nor was the UN secretary-general supposed to compromise himself to the point of being considered by the UK and the U.S. a surrogate agent for Argentina during the invasion of the Falklands; nor was another secretary-general entitled to use his position of influence to have the United States invade Somalia to capture and discredit a personal enemy; nor was the secretary-general to be so mixed up in African politics as to influence negatively the justified intervention of the UN to save five hundred thousand innocent Africans from being slaughtered, to fail to speak out in a timely manner against genocide in Darfur, nor to use a delayed declaration of the illegality of the Iraq war to influence an American presidential election. Nor should Kofi Annan also refer to murderers of innocent schoolchildren as "freedom fighters," even if he sympathizes with the use of terrorist tactics to achieve political ends.

How can these out-of-character roles for the UN Secretariat and its future secretaries-general be prevented? The easiest and biggest step that can be taken to ban the politicization of the Secretariat and the intervention of the UN secretary-general in local, national, or regional political issues is to establish a new order of openness and total transparency in all secretariat activities, not just with respect to budgetary issues. Everything that transpires in the Secretariat is not proprietary to the UN, nor secret. On the contrary, all the goings-on and activities that comprise the entire schedule of the Secretariat are the property—so to speak—of the UN's member states. Any UN member state should be able to demand and get a full accounting of what transpires in the Secretariat and is certainly entitled to object to inappropriate activity. The objection can properly be referred to the UN General Assembly, where the position of all the member states can be ascertained as to the propriety of the business transacted in the Secretariat.

That the apportionment of votes—one to each member state—is an absurd misrepresentation of the population of the world is another matter that also has to be resolved. Certainly all that makes openness in the conduct of the UN Secretariat's business no less desirable and urgent.

CHAPTER FOURTEEN

Can Internationalism Survive?

The U.S. government has consistently failed to take seriously repeated warnings that the UN Secretariat, the executive branch of the United Nations, has been and continues to be a breeding ground for corrupt practices, espionage activities, and politically oriented underground conspiracies. The UN Secretariat is not at present the neutral executor of the will of the majority of its member states within the lofty goals set forth by the UN Charter.

Lacking detailed information about conditions in the UN Secretariat, the U.S. Congress has always focused on a theme easy for American voters to understand—the waste of the resources provided to the UN by the U.S. Past Soviet intelligence operations have been of much less importance to Senate and House appropriations committees than these dollars-and-cents issues. Senate and House members have therefore focused on cutting the U.S. monetary contribution in order to solve all the ills of the UN. But they have not carried out their threats convincingly.

Different U.S. administrations have steered away from taking strong action to protest UN racism and anti-Semitism. They have refrained as well from examining the preposterous conflicts of interest in the UN Secretariat. On the contrary, on the pretext of getting along in a complex environment, the U.S. has permitted and in some cases encouraged the conflicts of interest and corruption that have progressively corroded it.

Can the United States afford to ignore the evidence of corruption, criminality, espionage, and political extremism that have been misguidedly tolerated at the UN? Or is this a necessary burden, the price we must pay for hosting a world forum? Is it, above all, a burden that the American people must not only tolerate, but pay for? What possible excuse can there be for not radically reforming an arcane system of diplomatic immunity so that the UN can clean up its act and play a more positive role in the world?

The U.S. and the USSR, acting in tacit alliance during the long years of the Cold War—when even as rivals they agreed on the irrelevance of the UN in a polarized world—are certainly the root cause of the prevalence of incompetence in the UN Secretariat and the repeated betrayal of its basic principles. However, the overriding issue now is that the congenitally corrupted Secretariat has acquired a new significance. Because of the tactics of massive destruction adopted by international terrorists, a complicit UN Secretariat incompetent to deal with such challenges looms as a potential threat to world order itself. The anti-Semitic scene in the UN Secretariat is rapidly turning into a broad-based anti-American bias, evidenced by the accurate reports of glee and celebration within the halls of the UN itself upon receipt of the news of the World Trade Center tragedy. In short, the UN is now a much bigger deal than the silly kindergarten sandbox arena that it amounted to before the 1990s.

Two statements were made during the UN General Assembly session of October 1, 2001, three weeks after September 11 and only two miles away from Ground Zero. When these statements were made, the General Assembly was struggling to define the difference between justified and unjustified terrorism.

First, the secretary-general spoke about a "need for moral clarity," signifying that not all terrorists were the same—some were real terrorists and others were freedom fighters. He did allow that the attack on the World Trade Center was the deliberate taking of innocent civilian life, "regardless of cause or grievance," but he did not clarify whether or not the attack upon the Pentagon, staffed mostly by military personnel, fell under the same classification.

Then the UN observer for Palestine, known as the PLO "ambassador," refined the issue further: "Issues of wars, armed conflict, foreign occupation, recognized as such by the international community . . . are governed by international humanitarian law, by Geneva conventions, so it's a different issue."

These were hardly diplomatic circumlocutions. They clearly implied that if a justifiable cause could be found for the World Trade Center massacre, it too would have to be regarded as an act perpetrated by freedom fighters pursuing a legitimate end. Terrorist actions have now been legitimized without challenge by the UN General Assembly in open debate.

Civilized society has proved vulnerable to forces that benefit from disorder, inefficiency, and corruption in international organizations. Neither the City of New York, the United States, nor the rest of the civilized world can afford to tolerate terrorist militants operating under the cover of UN immunity. Nor can bigoted intolerance be seen as a necessary evil that has to be tolerated even under the complex conditions that prevail during the give-and-take of international diplomacy.

Fortunately, most Americans now understand that international terrorism is not a cottage industry, but a multifaceted, multipurpose, sophisticated relationship among many small groups, large organizations, governments, and other support elements that can operate under the protective cover of international organizations. To control and gradually eradicate forces that seek power by fostering chaos, we must insist that all shelters for organized terrorism be eliminated, particularly those that thrive in our midst under whatever pretext.

Cleaning up the UN Secretariat and insuring that its staff operates in a manner roughly consistent with civilized standards of ethics and morality should in no way interfere with the function of the UN as a world forum. On the contrary, Secretariat activities defined by the ethics and principles of the UN Charter should enhance the effectiveness of the UN and permit the successful implementation of that forum's programs.

The present secretary-general has appealed for support in controlling worldwide conflicts and in preventing the use of violence to accomplish ends that should be addressed instead by means of diplomacy. These calls to reason are laudable and should be supported by all Americans, whatever their political persuasion. But the UN must do much more than just issue well-meaning pronouncements. To help the UN accomplish its worthy objectives, the author therefore proposes the following simple but effective measures:

- that religious activities be kept out of the UN Secretariat, a lay organization, since such services are easily accessible to Secretariat staff outside the UN premises;
- that all forms of nepotism be strictly forbidden in the UN Secretariat and in UN specialized agencies;
- that strict conflict of interest regulations be adopted and enforced in the UN Secretariat at least as rigorously as they are in the U.S. government;
- that expressions of racism and anti-Semitism be forbidden in the UN Secretariat under penalty of expulsion for any offenders, including the secretary-general;
- that moonlighting activities and business deals by UN Secretariat staff during and after working hours be strictly forbidden, and that offenders be subject to termination of UN employment;
- that the UN Secretariat and its specialized agencies sever and forbid all contacts with international and local organized crime;
- that the Secretariat make available to any of the member states direct access to all accounting records and any other financial and budget documents;
- that all intelligence operations or internal political activities be effectively banned in the Secretariat and UN agencies;

- that an internal security committee be created to work closely with member state law enforcement agencies in seeking out criminal and terrorist activities in the UN Secretariat in New York and overseas, providing cooperation with and internal UN access to law enforcement organizations tracking individuals suspected of violating UN rules that prohibit criminal and terrorist activities; and finally,

- that current Secretariat staff members—including all top-level officials—involved in obvious conflict of interest and past illegal activities be immediately relieved of their posts.

Since the UN Secretariat does not have sufficient authority to guarantee due process, protection for the rights of individuals should be provided by a properly appointed judicial tribunal outside the UN.

Future Security Council membership and the role of a much more representative General Assembly are difficult questions. They involve re-thinking the need, significance, and function of a totally refurbished international organization, one that is not based on the principle of neo-imperialist control of the world by a few northern-tier countries. Reinventing this aspect of the UN will thus probably require structuring a confederation of regional alliances or mini-UNs.

The reform of the UN Secretariat, on the other hand, is not a difficult matter at all. It involves making the Secretariat and its agencies thoroughly accountable to the member states, and establishing such standards of conduct as can be found in the bylaws of organizations and government agencies throughout the civilized world. Such reforms can be put into effect as early as tomorrow.

Much has to be done to make the UN into an up-to-date organization capable of rising to meet the challenges of a fractious world. But the excuse that the UN is but the sum of the wishes of its member states will no longer do. Bona fide internationalists do not envisage a world dominated by despotic regimes and human rights violators.

In short, there will be no meaningful reform in the UN political arena until a formula is found to turn the organization into a true world forum devoted to the protection of the interests of all its members as well as to the promotion of economic growth and the elimination of famine, poverty, injustice, and disease throughout the world.

It is the sincere hope of some of the UN's most respected critics that the current absurdity of the UN becoming the nexus of opposition to the United States will not bloom into a permanent condition. It is certainly up to the United States to take more positive steps to prevent this fatal realignment, because if this drift is not checked, then the United Nations has a short future life expectancy. Such an outcome would not be in the best interests of American security, nor would it benefit the future of mankind. Let us hope our leaders have the wisdom to save the UN from itself before it is too late.

ACKNOWLEDGMENTS

First to my wife, Patricia, computer genius, instant producer of printed copy from illegible manuscripts, indefatigable front-line editor.

Not being used to those rare literary agents who become one with their authors, I have come to regard Lynne Rabinoff not as my agent but as my alter ego, who understands the subject of this book almost better than I, who can seek the best environment for its publication, and who constantly translates its urgency far better than I can, inhibited as I am by the straitjacket of imposed modesty. Among her many amazing accomplishments on my behalf was finding the right editor, Adam Bellow. Adam, a distinguished writer with abundant inherited talent, restrained me when I waxed too eloquent, stimulated me when I waned by being too succinct, but above all, penetrated this book's theme of official absurdity as if he had made, alongside of me, the ten-year trip I describe here.